MW00714243

Everything
You Need to Know (and More!)
About Getting Your Child
into Private School

Copyright © 2005 Jeanine Jenks Farley

10-Digit ISBN 1-59113-751-9
13-Digit ISBN 978-1-59113-751-1

All rights reserved. No part of this publication may be
reproduced, stored in a retrieval system, or transmitted in any
form or by any means, electronic, mechanical, recording or
otherwise, without the prior written permission of the author.

Printed in the United States of America.

The information in this book is provided as a convenience to its
audience and in no way warrants the performance,
acceptability, applicability, or legal standing of any of the links
and information contained herein.

The businesses and services included in this directory were in
operation at the time they were added to this book. They are
independent businesses and are not under the control of the
writer or publisher of this book.

We imply no guarantee of satisfaction with the services
rendered by the businesses listed herein.

Jeanine Jenks Farley
Visit me on the Web at http://www.jjfarley.com
Email me at jeanine554@yahoo.com

2005

Everything You Need to Know (and More!) About Getting Your Child into Private School:

A Guide for Parents of Elementary, Middle, and High School Students

Jeanine Jenks Farley

About the Author

Jeanine Jenks Farley is a freelance writer, who has written for and edited textbooks for more than twenty years. She grew up on the West Coast (mostly Oregon and Alaska), but has lived in the Northeast for the past twenty-five years. She has a young daughter, who just started attending a private school. In her spare time, Jeanine enjoys writing fiction, romping with her daughter, travel, and dining out with her family.

Dedication

To my husband and daughter,
for without them, there would be no book.

Contents

Introduction...xiii

Chapter 1 The Big Decision.. 1
  Some Advantages of Private Schools 2
  Simplify the Process.. 4

Chapter 2 It's August. Gather Information................. 8
  Peers, Friends, Acquaintances 8
  Go Online.. 10

Chapter 3 September: Contact Schools 13
  Buy a Special Calendar 14
  Keep a Phone Log... 14
  Contact Information Worksheet................................ 15
  School Checklist 17

Chapter 4 October Fairs and Open Houses.............. 18
  Attend School Fairs... 18
  It's Open House Season 18

Chapter 5 November: The Parent Interview and Tour........... 25
  How to Dress 25
  How to Prepare for the Interview 25
  Questions to Ask 28
  Should I Be Honest About My Child's Weaknesses?........... 30
  Interview Deadlines Worksheet................................ 32
  The Parent Tour... 33
  Parent Tour Worksheet 37

Chapter 6 December: The Dreaded Application....... 39
  How to Fill Out the Application 40
  Biographical Information 40

Essay Questions 42
The Photograph 47
Teacher Recommendations Worksheet 50
Personal References Worksheet 52
Student Questionnaires 53
Admissions Tests 53

Chapter 7 January: The Child Visit and Financial Aid 56
What to Expect 56
Student Visit Worksheet 60
Applying for Financial Aid 61
Financial Aid Checklist 66

Chapter 8 February: The Waiting Game 67
Hurry Up and Wait! 67
Early Acceptance Letters 68

Chapter 9 March: Letters Good and Bad 70
Wait Listing 70
Comparing Financial Aid Offers 72
Comparing Schools 72

Chapter 10 April: Your Decision Is Made (Finally!) 74
To Attend Summer Camp or Not? 74
Declining Other Offers 74

Chapter 11 May: The New School 76
Health (and Other) Forms 76
What to Do If You Did Not Get In 76
Rolling Admissions 77

Chapter 12 June: Summer Reading Lists (and More) 79
Rolling Admissions: Keep Trying 79

Chapter 13 July: Summer Camp 82
    Meet Teachers, Classmates, and Parents........................... 83

Chapter 14 August: Preparing for the New School................. 85
    Visit the School and Classroom....................................... 85
    Buy Clothes and Supplies.. 86

Chapter 15 Students with Special Needs 88
    Specialized Schools 88
    Mainstream Schools.. 89
    Narrowing Your Choices.. 91
    What Should I Expect After My Child Is Accepted? 92

Chapter 16 Gifted Children.. 94
    School Provisions That Help Gifted Students 96
    Topics to Discuss 97

Chapter 17 Boarding School? You've Got to Be Kidding! 99
    Why Are Boarding Schools Attractive?.............................. 99
    Types of Boarding Schools 100

Chapter 18 Help! How Do I Pay for This? 104
    Qualifying for Financial Aid... 104
    Financial Aid Resources 106

Glossary... 109

Resources.. 113
    Independent Schools 113
    Religious Schools... 116
    Resources by State 119
    Financial Aid Sources 141
    Children with Learning Difficulties................................ 143
    Gifted Children 146

Checklists and Worksheets 149

Index 159

Introduction

When we decided to look at private schools for our young daughter, we discovered that there were no books on the market that demystified for us the very complicated and time-consuming application process. So we muddled through the hard way—by trial and error.

Since then, so many people have asked me for advice on how to apply and what to expect during the application process that I have decided to put my ideas and experiences into writing. I hope this book helps you as you embark on your exhilarating journey to explore private school options for your child.

Jeanine Jenks Farley

Chapter 1
The Big Decision

There's no doubt about it. Research proves that the better your education the better you do in life. But private schools? They're expensive. They're elitist. They lack diversity. My kid wouldn't fit in. Do you think any of these statements are true? Read on. What you discover may happily surprise you.

You can't afford a private school? Then simply apply for financial aid. You'd be surprised at how generous some schools are with their financial aid. Often the more expensive the school, the larger its endowment and the more of its tuition is used to subsidize other students. For example, at Buckingham, Browne & Nichols school (an extremely competitive and expensive private school near Boston), people earning $200,000 per year have been awarded financial aid. About 20 percent of students who attend private schools receive some sort of financial aid.

So don't let money worries inhibit your dreams. Apply to the best schools, and apply for financial aid while you're at it. I don't know of even one parent who wasn't able to finance a child's education once that child got accepted into a great school. When your child gets accepted, you will find a way to make it work. It may be a struggle, and you may have to get a second job, but most parents find the sacrifices well worthwhile.

So now you're seriously thinking about sending your child to a private (also called an independent) school. It's an enormous amount of work to find the best fit. Choosing a school is time consuming (there are so many good ones out there). Applying to a school is exhausting. (Why can't they all use the same application?) The interviews and child visits and tours need to be arranged and fit into your busy schedule. The process can be more daunting than applying to college. But, if your child is accepted, the work is worth it. You feel confident that your child is getting a wonderful education from caring teachers at a school he or she adores.

Some Advantages of Private Schools

Many private schools spend a great amount of time helping their students get into good schools after graduation—whether that school be a middle school, a high school, or a college. They teach students good interviewing techniques and practice with them, including such simple things as firmly shaking hands, making eye contact, talking loudly enough, sounding confident and friendly, appearing poised, and so on. They help students learn and practice how to write a good essay, they prepare them for any standardized tests they have to take, they help them evaluate schools for which they might be a good fit, they write excellent recommendations, and so on. All of these things can give private school students an edge over public school students when it comes time to move on to a school at the next level.

In addition, private schools provide many other benefits. Some public schools share some of these qualities, but many do not.

1. Private schools usually have a low student/teacher ratio, which means that your child gets more individual attention and the teacher will have more time to individualize instruction. This is especially helpful if your child is very smart, has unusual interests or talents, or has special learning needs.
2. Private school curriculums are often a year or more ahead of public school curriculums. Private schools cover more ground (and often have a longer day) than public schools. In

addition, private school students do more homework and watch less television than public school students.

3. Teachers in private schools are often passionate about what they do. You can see this in the way they interact with the students. This passion for learning is passed on to the students, who also become passionate about learning and school.

4. Private schools feel very safe. Parents drop their children off every morning, and they don't worry about them during the day. The environment is warm, nurturing, and secure. Students feel safe both physically and emotionally.

5. Private schools value parental input. They encourage parents to work with their students at home, but also they encourage parents to participate in school activities and events. Parents' ideas are welcome and valued because parents are as much a part of the school as the students are.

6. Children at private schools are more physically active than public school students. Many private schools require participation in sports, and, at the very least, they provide plenty of opportunities for children to become involved in a physical activity that they enjoy.

7. Private schools have high expectations for their students and a culture that reinforces achievement. Being a hard worker or outstanding in math are both qualities that are admired and encouraged at private schools. At private schools everyone is expected to work hard, and everyone is expected to succeed.

8. Private schools emphasize morals, decent behavior, and good citizenship. Most schools provide opportunities for students to become involved in community projects or partnerships.

9. Private schools have clear expectations and limits. In addition, students are expected to be responsible for their

own behavior. By the time they are in middle school, private school students are expected to spend their evenings doing homework, to contribute to school clubs or sports, and to participate in class.

10. Private schools become one's family and community. Students spend so much time on academic and extracurricular activities at the school, and the parents spend so much time at the school supporting their students, that the school becomes the family's second home.

The Process Can Be Fun

Although the process of applying to private schools can be daunting, it can be exciting, too. There are so many wonderful schools out there that your chances of finding one you adore and that is a good fit for your child are very good. Your hardest problem many be sifting through the alternatives and narrowing your choices. How do you decide which features of a school are most important when all the schools sound so inviting?

Look at the process as an adventure. You are exploring a new and irresistible world—a world that can lead to an exciting and compelling educational experience for your child.

Tip: *Something about the difficulty of applying to a private school doesn't seem quite right, especially if your child is only four years old. But you gain much in exchange for your hard work—a wonderful educational experience for your child. This book will simplify the process for you. It's really not as hard as it seems.*

Simplify the Process

If the process of applying to a private school seems overwhelming and complicated, relax. This book will guide you through each step you need to take. If you focus on one small step at a time, the process is much easier. So break the process down. Make lists of what you need to do week by week. Then do one or two things on your list each day. See! Before you know it, you will be relaxing on the back porch drinking mint juleps while you wait for acceptance letters to arrive from your favorite schools.

The application process can be broken down by month. Here, roughly, is what you will need to do the year before your child enrolls in a private school:

August: Compile a broad list of nearby private schools.
September: Call schools and request information packets.
October: Attend open houses and school fairs.
November: Schedule parent interviews and tours of the schools.
December: Complete and send in the applications to the schools you like most.
January: Schedule child visits. Send in financial aid information.
February: Wait! Relax. Drink mint juleps.
March: Receive acceptance (and rejection) letters.
April: Decide which school to attend. Send a deposit. Decide whether or not to attend summer camp at the new school.
May: Develop an alternative plan if you did not get in to a school. Some schools have rolling admissions, so it is still not too late to get into a less-competitive school. If you did get accepted, fill out health forms, emergency contact forms, and billing information.
June: Receive from the new school summer reading lists and work packets. Apply, visit, and interview at schools with rolling admissions, if needed.
July: Attend summer camp at the new school. Enroll in extended day or after-school programs.

August: Prepare for the new school year. Buy school clothes and supplies. Meet teachers and visit classrooms. Prepare your child for the new school year. Receive from the school a map, a welcome letter from the head of school, a parent handbook, a school calendar, information about the parents' association, athletic program information, information about field trips, and so on.

Is It Hard to Get In?

Some independent schools are hard to get into. Some may have only a few openings for a hundred or more children. Do you even have a chance of getting in? Yes. Especially if you know what you are doing. This book will tell you what you need to know to enhance your chances of being accepted—not just anywhere but at one of your top-choice schools.

Tip: What Do Schools Want in a Child? *Almost every school wants to enroll children who are curious and eager to learn. You will hear this over and over. Make sure you present an example or two in your interview and application that shows these qualities in your child.*

In addition, even though they may not tell you this, schools are also looking for children who show leadership ability or unusual aptitude in academics, the arts, or athletics. If your child excels in one of these areas, you should be certain to emphasize these qualities.

Because schools are looking for diversity and balance in their classrooms, there is not one quality or ability that schools seek. They want some children who are energetic and outgoing and some who are quieter and more introspective. They want some children who are intense and focused and some who are broad in their interests. In general, they want children with a good attitude. So don't worry that your child doesn't possess the right skills or talents or energy level. Schools want a broad

6

range of skills and talents and energy levels, and your child may be just the type to bring a nice balance to the classroom.

Tip: What Do Schools Want from Parents? *Schools want parents who will participate in their child's education and be a part of the school community. In short, they want parents who are involved! Make sure you mention in your interviews and application how much you want to become involved in the school community. If you have skills that you would like to share with kids or the school community, mention this. If you'd like to read stories to young students, head a committee, work on a newsletter or advertising, let the school know. Many private schools need the advice of lawyers, engineers, or financial experts. They could use the skills of carpenters or landscapers. Offer your skills and expertise. And then make sure you follow through. Don't offer something that you will not have time to provide.*

Chapter 2
It's August. Gather Information.

T hink about what type of school you want to send your child to. There are two main categories of schools: religious schools and nonreligious schools. About 25 percent of the nation's schools are nonsectarian, meaning they are not affiliated with any religion. These private schools (often called independent schools) may be academically challenging and provide a strong moral education.

Many parents want their students to be taught in a school that supports their faith. There are many Catholic, Protestant, Quaker, and Jewish schools across the country. There are also Muslim schools, and schools that teach other faiths. If you are interested in a religious school, talk first to your religious leader about local options. Most of these private schools have a traditional academic workload along with religion courses and mandatory church attendance.

One half of all private school students in this country attend Catholic schools. Some students attend because of the religious training, but many students who attend Catholic schools are not even Catholic! Parents may send their children to these schools if they perceive the education is better, the schools are safer, discipline is better, and so on.

Peers, Friends, Acquaintances

What's the first step in selecting a school? First, you need to find out what schools are out there. Begin your search in the summer. Ask everyone you meet if they know of any good private schools nearby. What do they like about the school? Pick their brains. Ask your doctor, lawyer, and neighbors. Begin listing schools that people recommend.

Then think about what type of school you are looking for. What characteristics of a school are important to you? What are your child's interests? Are you looking for a school that is strong in the arts? athletics? academics? moral values? languages? religious instruction? discipline? special needs assessment? gifted learning?

Begin listing the characteristics that are most important to you. This will help you analyze the schools that you hear about.

What Is a Montessori School?

In 1896, Maria Montessori became the first female physician in Italy. Ten years later, she gave up her medical practice to work with young children. Her scientific observations of children led her to develop the Montessori method. Some features of a Montessori education include the following:

- Most Montessori schools enroll young children, from preschool to about sixth grade.
- Children normally stay in the same class for three years. Each child learns at her own pace. The age range allows gifted children the stimulation of intellectual peers without requiring that they skip a grade or feel out of place.
- Hands-on learning is emphasized.
- Each manipulative has a step-by-step procedure for being used and focused toward a specific learning concept. For example, math counting rods are not to be transformed into the walls of a building. Each child works independently on a small rug doing a task different from the other children.
- Children learn everyday tasks such as pouring, sweeping, and tying.
- The curriculum emphasizes sight, sound, touch, taste, and smell.

What Is a Waldorf School?

Rudolf Steiner (1861 to 1925) created the method of instruction common to Waldorf schools. Some features of a Waldorf education include the following:

- Kindergarten has no academics. Minimal academics is found in first grade. Reading is not taught until second or third grade.
- From grades one to eight, students have one teacher who stays with the same class for the entire eight years.
- Art, music, gardening, and foreign languages (usually two in elementary grades) are central. All children learn to play the recorder and to knit.
- There are no textbooks in the first through fifth grades. Children have workbooks that they fill in during the year.
- Learning is noncompetitive. No grades are given in elementary school.
- The use of television and computers by young children are discouraged.
- The main subjects are taught for two to three hours per day for three to five weeks.

Go Online

Several web sites can help you find schools in your area that match your needs.

1. The Department of Education (DOE) in most states has lists of all schools, public and private. If you visit your DOE web site, you can probably obtain a list of all the private schools in your state, listed alphabetically by school name (that is, not sorted by town, which would be most convenient). So it may be a little cumbersome to sort through the list, but when you do, you should have a good idea of the schools that are nearby.

2. Visit http://www.greatschools.net. This site provides you with information about all the schools in an area you choose, both public and private. You can narrow your focus by region or type of school. You will learn how large the school is, what type of school it is (elementary, middle, high), whether it is public or private, and sometimes how difficult it is to be accepted. This site also provides contact information, so you can visit the web sites of schools or call for more information. Write down the contact information of any school that seems to meet your needs.
3. Visit the web site of the National Association of Independent Schools (http://www.nais.org). The site can help you locate many independent schools in your area. However, it will not be a comprehensive list because not every private school is a member of this organization. Look at this site to begin compiling a list of schools that fit your needs. (Are you looking for a day school or a boarding school? a coed school? a school in your town? an elementary school? a high school?) Once you have a list of schools that sound like good possibilities, go to the web site of each school. Read about the school. Does the school sound like a good fit for your child? Where is the school? If the school is two hours away, do you really want to make the commute every day?
4. Visit http://www.parochial.com if you are interested in a parochial school. This site has links to parochial schools by state.
5. Visit the web site of your city or town and nearby cities and towns. Many of these sites have compiled a list of the schools in the community, both public and private.
6. Use a search engine to locate the type of school you are interested in. For example, if you want to find out about all of the Montessori schools near you, simply type "Montessori

schools in (state)." You should be presented with a list of the schools in your area.

Drive bys

Take a drive by the schools you have selected. What do the schools look like from the outside? Is there adequate parking for dropping off children? Are the buildings well-maintained or run down? Are there playing fields? basketball or tennis courts? a pool? Is the school large or small? Are there trees and grass? asphalt and traffic? How noisy is the area? Are there industries nearby that pollute the air?

How long does it take to drive to the school? Will you feel comfortable driving this distance twice a day? What if you get sick? Will you be able to make alternate arrangements for your child to get to school? Is there bus service in the area?

Complete a Broad List

Make of list of all the schools you are interested in. Include phone numbers. Cast your net wide at this point. You don't want to eliminate schools for minor reasons just yet.

Chapter 3
September: Contact Schools

E arly in September, call, write, fax, or email the schools you have put on your list. Request an information packet. (If you call earlier than September, the schools will send you materials from the previous year, and you will have to call again in September anyway.) Soon a large envelope will arrive in your mailbox. It will usually include the following:

- A glossy brochure or view book about the school. It will likely show happy children in sunlit classrooms and playing fields. It will also include information about the school, its programs, curriculum, and wonderful faculty.
- An application for admission.
- A list of deadlines. This list will tell you when the application is due, as well as when parent interviews, tours, and child visits should be completed. It will also list when teacher and personal recommendations are due, when any tests or entrance exams are due, and on and on. It can be overwhelming to think about all you have to do and the short timeframe in which you must accomplish it all. But take it slowly. Focus on one task at a time. Begin by getting out a calendar and marking on it all the deadlines. Do this for every school you are interested in.
- Information about open houses. Open houses are important. Mark the dates and time on your calendar. Attend each open house to find out if the school seems like a good fit for you and your child.

Buy a Special Calendar

To help keep track of all the deadlines, some people find it useful to buy a calendar and post it near the telephone. You can list important dates and deadlines on the calendar, such as open houses and application deadlines. As you continue with the process, you can list interviews and tours, child visits, financial aid deadlines, recommendation letter deadlines, test deadlines, and so on. All this information will take up a lot of space on your calendar, so it is usually best to have one calendar dedicated solely to the private school admissions process.

Keep a Phone Log

It is also useful to keep a phone log near the telephone. A spiral notebook works well. In this notebook, you will keep records of your telephone calls to the schools. You may want to have a separate page for each school. Write down the date and time of each call, to whom you talked (and in what department), and the information they supplied. You can also use this log to keep track of questions you have for people at each school.

The notebook will help you greatly when you need to make calls because you will have contact names and phone numbers right at your fingertips. You will not have to rifle through view books and brochures and other literature to find the names and phone numbers that you need.

In the beginning (or at the back) of your phone log, you may want to create a list of contacts for each school that looks something like this:

Contact Information Worksheet

School Name:

Admissions contact:

Title:

Address:

Address:

Phone:

Fax:

Email:

Financial Aid contact:

Title:

Address:

Address:

Phone:

Fax:

Email:

Get Organized

You may also find it helpful (I did) to make a list of all the deadlines for each school. After you have completed each item on your list (one list for each school), write the date the item was completed, and cross it off your list. You may find great satisfaction in crossing items off your list as the process continues. You will feel a sense of immense accomplishment when you look back and realize how much you have done. A sample checklist is shown:

School Checklist

Name of School:

Item	Date Due	Date Completed
☐ Parent visit, tour, interview		
☐ Application and fee		
☐ Financial statement		
☐ Child visit		
☐ ISEE or SSAT scores		
☐ Family history form		
☐ Personal reference 1		
☐ School report		
☐ Teacher recommendation 1		
☐ Teacher recommendation 2		
☐ Child's essay		
☐ W-2s and tax forms		
☐ Admission letters mailed		
☐ Parent reply date		

Chapter 4
October Fairs and Open Houses

A school fair is an event in which all of the independent schools in a state or region come together in one location to provide information about their schools to prospective parents and students. Representatives from each school can be found. You will be able to talk to representatives from many schools, collect literature, and take notes. You may find some schools represented that you didn't even know existed. Sometimes one of these new or lesser-known schools can be a perfect fit for your child.

Attend School Fairs

To find out when a school fair is scheduled, call a private school near you and ask when the next school fair will be. In some states, there will be several school fairs with schools from a given region at each fair. If you live in a location that is on the border between two regions, you may want to attend fairs in more than one region. For example, there might be a fair for a region just north of you and another fair for the region you are in. But many of the schools in the region north of you are closer than some of the schools in your region. If this is the case, you may feel it necessary to attend both fairs.

When you get back from the fair, read all of the literature you have collected. Do some of the schools appeal to you? If they do, you probably will want to attend an open house at these schools.

It's Open House Season

All schools have open houses. Holding an open house is a good method of advertising. If you are one of those people who doesn't like clicking through all of the screens on a web site to find out the date and time of an open house, just call the school. Ask them when their open houses are scheduled. Find out if children are welcome. Mark the time and date on your calendar.

Tip: *Some people worry about the cost of an independent school. It's true, these schools are expensive, but price should not be your first concern. Most schools have at least some financial aid available, so don't eliminate any school yet because of the cost.*

Fact-Finding Missions

Open houses are your fact-finding missions. You actually visit the school and see what the buildings and facilities look like. You meet teachers and administrators and other parents. You ask many, many questions.

The first open houses are held every fall. Try to attend open houses in the fall the year before your child will enroll. Some open houses have lectures for parents to attend. Others allow you to arrive and stroll through the school at your own speed. Some have parent-led tours. Others have tours led by administrators. You will usually have an opportunity to talk to people in the admissions department. All open houses have refreshments.

Do I Bring My Child?

At most open houses, children are welcome. Very young children will have little or no interest in the talks, but it's important to bring them anyway. They are the ones who will be attending the school. It's important to gauge their reactions to the place.

If you have a very young child, try to find the classrooms for children of that age. There you will find age-appropriate toys for your child, and teachers who can talk to you about what the school is like for young children. This is also an opportunity to scope out the school. If one parent or adult stays with the young child in the classroom, another parent or adult can tour the school to see the big picture.

The child in the classroom will be familiarizing herself with the school. If she needs to return to the school at a later date for a child visit, this early visit can help ease the way. It's possible she will even visit the same room! Before the child visit, you can remind your child of the layout of the room, what the teacher was like, or of some of her favorite toys in the room. (If you are lucky, those toys will still be there on your return.)

The Small Picture:
The Child's Classroom

This is a good opportunity for a parent to find out about classroom life. What's the student-teacher ratio? How long is the class day? What happens during a typical day? If you are extremely lucky, you or your child may develop a rapport with a teacher. If you are even more lucky (and this does happen sometimes), this teacher may have a role in selecting which students are admitted to her classroom. At the very least, you are helping your child prepare for the day when he or she will have to return to the school for the dreaded child visit. (There will be more on the child visit in a later chapter.)

The Big Picture:
Looking Around the School

As you tour the school, notice the layout of the rooms. Are desks lined up in rows, or are there tables arranged in circles? Do the classrooms seem friendly and inviting? Is the school itself towering and imposing or cozy and intimate? What facilities are there for science, computers, art, shop, music, athletics, languages?

Is there student work on display throughout the building? Do the teachers seem excited and energized when they talk about the students and the school? Are the classrooms well supplied? Do they seem organized or chaotic? Which would your child prefer?

After you tour the school, you will probably be excited and pleased with what you see. You may wish that there had been schools like this when you were a child. Now, while things are still fresh in your mind, jot down what you liked most and least about the school. Over time, and after many school visits, the distinctions between schools may become fuzzy in your mind. So while everything is fresh, make a few notes about the most important details of the school. You can write your notes in the back of your phone log if you want to keep everything at your fingertips.

My Story: *When I first started visiting schools, I did not like parent-led tours. I wanted to tour with an administrator who would have some say in the admissions decision. But over time, I realized how valuable other parents were. You can ask them questions you cannot ask teachers or administrators. You can ask them how many schools they applied to, how hard it was to get into the school, what the school is looking for in a new student, the pros and cons of the school, and who makes the admissions decisions. You can ask them what to expect during the child visit: Is it a large group or a small group? How long is the visit? Where are the parents during the visit? What questions do they ask the child? Parents who have been through the process before you can help you get a sense of the school and its expectations.*

Meet Other Parents

If you are lucky enough to meet a parent, and many schools invite parents to help show off the school, you can pump him or her for information. Ask the parent what steps they took to get admitted. How many schools they applied to? What goes on during the child visit? Who makes the admissions decisions? Is it one person? two? three? Try to remember who the decision-makers are. You may bump into them during this visit or another visit.

Ask the parents what qualities the school looks for in a child. (You probably won't get a clear answer to this question, since schools look for many different qualities, but if you ask this question of many parents, you may get a sense that the school leans more heavily toward one type of student than another.) Ask what the parent's children are like and what their favorite aspects of the school are. Ask about what occurs during a typical day, what town the family lives in, if kids or families socialize outside of school, and so on.

When you are done talking to the parent, make a note of his or her name. The parent is probably someone active in the school community and well-known to the administrators. You may find an occasion to talk to this person again, or to describe the person's enthusiasm to administrators.

Meet the Teachers

These are the people your child will be dealing with every day. Try, in particular, to meet the teacher or teachers who will be teaching your child (assuming she gets in). If your child is young, let the child play in the classroom or classrooms where children of that age are taught. This allows your child to become familiar with the room and may make the upcoming child visit less threatening; in addition, it allows the teacher or teachers to get to know your child informally. It's possible your child will make a better impression under these circumstances than during the chaos of a child visit—especially if it is a visit in which there are sixteen kids and thirty-two parents and nine teachers crammed together in one classroom. Any child could be overwhelmed in such a crowded and noisy environment.

Meet the Administrators

The administrators run the school. The Head of Admissions or other people in the admissions office may decide whether or not your child is admitted. The head of the school and certain teachers may also have a say in who is admitted. If you don't know who is making the decisions, it is best to assume everyone has a role in the process.

You can ask administrators what they are looking for in candidates to their school. It is wise to tell them how much you like the school and how impressed you are with the parents and children you have already met. If the children in the school seem poised and confident, look you directly in the eye, and shake hands firmly, mention this to the administrators. Tell them how impressed you are by this behavior (assuming you are impressed). Tell them how friendly and committed the parents seem or how passionate and dedicated the teachers seem. (Don't lie, however. Describe the qualities you've seen and admire. It shouldn't be hard to notice some very good qualities of the students, teachers, and children. If you don't notice anything positive, perhaps this is not the best school for your child, or perhaps you are not seeing a representative sample. Keep looking.)

Tip: Does applying for financial aid diminish your chances of acceptance? *Usually financial aid decisions are made independently of admissions decisions, so applying for aid does not diminish your chances of acceptance. Rarely (but this does happen), applying to more than one school will affect your chances of financial aid. One school sent us a notice which said, in effect, that if we applied to more than one school, we would not be eligible for financial aid in the first round in March. We* *would be eligible for aid in the second round (in May) but there were no guarantees that there would be any money left by then.*

This policy, I assume, was to discourage people from applying to more than one school, but since this school had only three openings the year before, we had no choice but to apply to other schools. We really liked the school, but we knew that we would probably not get financial aid—at least during the first year—if we were accepted at this school.

If you are accepted at a school like this, you will have to weigh whether or not you can afford to pay full tuition the first year, and whether or not you think you can get financial aid in future years. It is best to be prepared to pay the full tuition each year. If you do eventually get financial aid, you will be in better shape than you had hoped. If you don't get financial aid, well, at least you are prepared for that contingency.

Narrowing the Focus

After you've attended open houses, you may be able to identify some schools that you do not think would be a good fit for your child. Good. Cross those schools off of your list, especially if your list is long. Applying to three, four, or five schools is about all anyone can handle reasonably. We applied to six schools, but got so overwhelmed by January that we came very close to dropping one of the schools.

Chapter 5
November: The Parent Interview and Tour

Almost every school will want to interview either the parents or the child or both. If the child is young, then the parents will schedule an interview and a tour of the school. If the child is entering middle school or high school, an interview with the child may be scheduled. These child interviews will be discussed in detail in chapter 7. Here we will discuss how parents can prepare for their interview and tour.

How to Dress

Since most parent interviews occur during the work day, many parents will simply put on their office clothes and wear these to the interview. This type of clothing is perfectly acceptable at an interview. If you wear casual clothes to work or you work from home, wear something that looks respectful, such as nice pants, a sweater, and leather shoes. You don't need to don a business suit if you don't normally wear one, but you do need to dress as if you respect the process.

If you work in a lab, an auto body shop, a farm, do road construction, or other dirty work, you will probably not want to wear your work clothes to the interview. If you are stopping for the interview on your way to work, bring your work clothes with you. You can change into them after the interview when you arrive at work. Again, try to appear respectful of the interview process. The interviewer wants to see from your appearance that you take the process seriously.

How to Prepare for the Interview

Some interviewers are better than others. They will ask you good questions, take copious notes, and make you feel as if they really care about you and your child. When the interview is concluded, you will feel as if you and your child have been understood, and you will feel as if the information you imparted will reach the people who make the all-important admissions decisions.

It's always good to interview with a person who will be part of the team who makes the admissions decision, but this is not always possible, and sometimes you don't even know who makes the decisions. Sometimes you will interview with a person who asks superficial questions, who doesn't seem to have a good feel for you or your child, who is not making the decisions, who doesn't take notes, and who is likely not going to pass on important information to the decision makers. There's nothing you can do about this except to be prepared for it.

Before you go to an interview, list on paper or in your mind three important points you want to make about your child (use anecdotes or little stories to show these characteristics, if possible). If the interviewer is not good at eliciting information from you, you will have to make sure you interject your three points. If the interviewer doesn't ask, you can simply say something like, "May I tell you what my child is like?" Then list the three most important things about your child. You may want to think of an example showing your child's curiosity (schools look for children who are curious and eager to learn), perhaps his or her intelligence or imagination, and an example of his or her verbal or mathematical or mechanical or artistic (or whatever) ability.

Some questions the interviewer may ask you include the following:

- What are your child's least or favorite activities or subjects? Although you want to paint a favorable impression of your child, it is important to be honest. After all, you are looking for a good fit for your child, and if the school doesn't have an accurate view of your

child, it might be difficult to find a place where your child feels like he or she fits in.
- What books does your child like?
- What are your child's social skills like?
- What are your child's weaknesses? What areas would you like the school to work on with your child?
- Does your child learn better with or without lots of structure?
- What do you (the parents) do for a living?
- What are you looking for in a school?
- Why does this school appeal to you?
- What type of discipline do you use at home?

It's good to review the school's web site and viewbook before the interview, so you can talk about the school's strengths and why you think the school might be a good fit for your child.

Try to schedule interviews early—in November or December. You will have a greater choice of dates and times, so you will be able to better fit the interview into your schedule. If you put the interview off until January, there will be fewer slots available. You may have to take a date and time that is not convenient to you. (Some people think that scheduling an interview later is better because the interview will be fresher in the minds of the admissions personnel. My sense is that when the interview is conducted does not make a great deal of difference because our child was admitted to schools at which we interviewed both early and late. The schools seemed able to recall the highlights of our interview whenever it was conducted.)

Remember, children do not come to the parent interview. So you need to make plans for what to do with your child or children. If the child is in school, preschool, or day-care, you can schedule the interview for a time when your child is already away from you. If not, you will have to arrange for a baby-sitter or other child care.

My Story: *I put one school interview off until January. The only day and time available was on a Tuesday at 1 P.M. My daughter attended preschool Monday, Wednesday, and Friday mornings. So Tuesday afternoon was not a good time. But there was nothing I could do. We scheduled a baby-sitter, but she canceled at the last minute. What could we do? The deadline for completing interviews was a day away. We could not postpone. We decided that my husband would stay home with our young daughter, and I would attend the interview. It's best if both parents attend the interview, but most schools are accommodating if only one parent can attend. I went to the interview. It went well. Our daughter was accepted into the school. But if I had it to do over again, I would schedule that interview for November or December.*

Questions to Ask

The interview has two purposes: The school wants to find out about you and your child, but also, you want to find out if the school is a good fit for your child. With that in mind, here are some types of questions you may want to ask:

- What is the focus of the school? Is it academic, artistic, athletic? How much of each day do students spend participating in each of these types of activities?
- What are the strengths of this school?
- What are the weaknesses of this school?
- How flexible is the school? That is, what happens if a first-grade child is working at a fourth-grade level in math? What happens if a fourth-grade child is having trouble with reading comprehension? What happens if a prekindergarten child already knows how to read?

Think about your child's academic, social, and emotional traits. How will the school handle your child's strengths and weaknesses?

- What is the student/teacher ratio? Usually, the fewer students per teacher, the more individual attention a child will receive.
- How long have the teachers been at this school? You are looking for a school at which the teacher turnover is low. A low turnover means the teachers are happy with the school, and the parents and school are happy with the teachers.
- Where do graduates of this school go? If graduates are accepted at competitive schools, you can feel somewhat confident that the quality of the education is high.
- At what age do students learn a foreign language? compete in sports? take drama? Ask about whatever aspects of the curriculum are important to you and your student.
- How long is the school day? Is there an extended day or after-school option? What happens during this time?
- What clubs and extracurricular activities can my child participate in?
- How can parents get involved in the school community?
- What is the school's philosophy and vision for its students?
- Is the school accredited? Is it affiliated with any universities?
- Do students take field trips? Where do they go and what do they learn?
- How much is the tuition? What other fees are there?
- How much time are children expected to spend on homework?
- How often are standardized tests given? What are the purposes of the tests?

- What is the school's approach to discipline? What methods do they use to modify a child's behavior?
- How many openings are there? How many applications for those spaces does the school usually receive?

Diversity

Do you feel like you don't fit in? Relax! Schools like diversity. Being different can be to your advantage. If your background is different from most, you may be a welcome addition to the school. Proudly discuss your background. Make your life sound interesting and compelling. Chances are others will find it interesting and compelling, too.

- Does someone in your family speak a language other than English? That's great! Tell the school about it.
- Is someone in your family from another country? Great! Tell the school.
- Are you from a working-class background? Don't hide it. Be proud of your work ethic. Describe your family values.

Should I Be Honest About My Child's Weaknesses?

Sometimes interviewers will ask you to describe your child's weaknesses, faults, or areas in which the child could improve. Don't volunteer weaknesses, but have something in mind to discuss in case you are asked this question. Try to reply in a way that describes a typical problem for a child of that age. Also mention that the child is improving in the area.

My Story: *When asked to describe one of my three-year-old daughter's weaknesses, I told a story about a time she was playing with her good friend in the library. The two had been playing together well for a couple of hours. As noon approached,* *the two were getting tired and hungry. My daughter told her friend to sit in a specific chair. The friend started crying because she did not like being spoken to in a bossy tone. Then my daughter started crying because she had not meant to hurt her friend's feelings. So we ended up with two crying children, who did not have the social skills to express themselves in a more diplomatic fashion. I explained to the interviewer that although my daughter tries, she could at times use some help learning to be more diplomatic. She's learning, but it's sometimes hard for her to remember how others feel when she speaks.*

Interview Deadlines

You can use a worksheet like the one that follows to help you keep track of your interview deadlines.

Interview Deadlines Worksheet

Interviews must be completed by the following dates.

	Latest Date	**Date Completed**
School 1:		
School 2:		
School 3:		
School 4:		
School 5:		
School 6:		

The Parent Tour

After the interview, you will often be led on a tour of the school. This is your opportunity to ask more questions, and to see the school with students in attendance. Sometimes a school administrator will lead this tour; sometimes it will be a parent. If it is an administrator, you can continue to ask questions about the school. If it is a parent, you can ask questions about the admissions process itself, such as

- Who makes the admissions decisions? Are teachers involved, or is it only the admissions personnel?
- What happens during the child visit?
- How many schools did you apply to? Which ones did you like most, and why?
- What are your children like? Why is this school a good fit for them?
- How does the school handle problems between children?
- Do parents and children socialize together after school? You may hear about Friday afternoon ski trips, carpools, play dates, drama performances. Or you may realize that the students come from so far away that most are not able to get together outside of school.

Think about how your child would fit in to the classrooms you see. When you look in on classrooms, try to identify a child with a temperament like your own. How does that child seem to like the classroom?

The Teachers

Notice the teachers.

- Do they seem approachable and friendly?
- Do they seem to know the subject matter?
- If they are teaching a foreign language, are they native speakers?

- Is the language class conducted in English or in the language being learned?
- Are the math and science classes lectures or hands-on experiences?
- How do the teachers act in the halls, outside of the classroom? Do they seem happy and energized? Tired and bored?
- Do the teachers know the names of the students in the halls?
- In the classroom, do they elicit volunteers or call on students by name?

The Facilities

Notice the facilities.

- Do you think your child would be happy with the gym or the pool or the playing fields?
- Would your child like the auditorium or art or music classrooms?
- What musical instruments are available to learn?
- What dance or drama or acting facilities are there?
- What exciting, new things can your child try?
- If there is a computer room, is there a computer for every student?
- Are the science labs new or dilapidated?
- Do you see student work throughout the school?
- Does the school give the impression that students should not touch things?

Things to Notice in the Classroom

You want a school that will help your child grow and develop as a person. As you visit classrooms, notice what the students are like.

- Are they happy? engaged?
- Do they work alone? in a group?

- Is the setting quiet? loud?
- Do children move around in the classroom, or do they sit still?
- Are desks lined up in rows?
- Do children work in groups at tables or stations?
- Does the teacher lecture in the front?
- Do students sit in a circle around the teacher?
- Are students encouraged to ask questions, or do they mostly listen?

Your Child

Think about your child. How do you think your child would fit in in this environment.

- Would the school do a good job of drawing out your shy child?
- Would it be able to channel the energy of your active child?

Religious Schools

Exception: If you are applying to a religious school, think carefully before you reveal anything about your background that flies in the face of church doctrine. Don't discuss any opinions you hold that are too different. In fact, avoid discussing controversial issues altogether if you can, especially if you know that your opinions are different from the views of the church or the school.

What do you do if you want to send your child to a religious school, but you don't agree with every tenet of the religion? Relax! It's probably impossible for any person to agree with every tenet of a religion. As long as you feel comfortable with the religion overall, you needn't sweat the small stuff.

However, if you foresee a major difference, a teaching so profound that you cannot live with it, you have two choices:

- Find another school.

- Work for change within the school (and even within the religion). This may be difficult, and you may not be successful. The time commitment may be extensive. You may find yourself leaving the school down the road. So think carefully about whether or not you want to pursue this course.

Only you can weigh the pros and cons here. But try to keep your child's welfare foremost in mind. This is not about you. You are trying to find a school in which your child will thrive and blossom and grow.

Use a worksheet like the following to help you collect data while on a parent tour of the school.

Parent Tour Worksheet

School:
Address:
Contact/Phone:

Grades served (K to 8, 9 to 12):

Total number of students:

Total students in grade you are applying for:

Grade foreign language instruction begins:

Other instruction:

Extracurricular activities:

Extended day/after-school program:

Sports/athletics:

Facilities:

Arts instruction:

Teachers seemed:

Students seemed:

School seemed:

How school is unique:

Best qualities of school:

Worst qualities of school:

The Thank-You Letter

After you've completed the tour and interview, it is important to send a thank-you letter. (Some schools will send you a thank-you letter, too.) In the letter, thank the interviewer for taking the time to speak with you. Explain how much you like the school and what a good fit you believe it would be for your child. If the interviewer did not take notes or if the interviewer is not the one making the admissions decisions, you may want to briefly include the three most important points about your child. With a little luck, the thank-you note will make it into your child's application folder. If the interviewer did take notes, you may want to include one additional brief example of a special quality your child possesses. You do not want to reiterate everything you said in the interview.

Keep your thank-you letter brief and friendly. People like to be thanked for their work, but they don't want to be pestered by an overbearing parent.

Chapter 6
December: The Dreaded Application

The private school admissions application can be intimidating. After all, you want to make a good impression. You want your child to stand out from the crowd. You want the application to be so wonderful that the admissions committee will have no choice but to admit your deserving child.

So how to begin? First, make a copy (or two) of the application. Use these as practice applications. Only after the practice application is perfect will you fill out the real application.

Important Skills

Some people like interviewing. Others like writing. But both are important in this process. If you are weak in one of these areas, work to improve your skills.

If your writing skills are less than stellar, have someone proofread your application before you send it in. Correct any mistakes. Make the application look professional. Make it look as if you care.

Where to Begin

The easiest way to begin is simply to break the process down. Think about one question and answer at a time. After you have finished the entire application, reread it. Think about the big picture. What do you want the school to know about your child that you haven't already mentioned? Revise your application to include your new ideas. Then neatly copy your answers onto the real application.

How to Fill Out the Application

If you have several applications, start with the one that is due first (this is often the most difficult application for the most prestigious school). After you have answered all of the questions on this application, you will find that most of the questions on the other applications will be variations of the ones you have already answered. Once you have the first application completed, the others are easier to complete.

Biographical Information

First, the application will ask for biographical information (applicant's name, address, and school; parents' names, addresses, and employers). These questions are usually straightforward and easy to answer. But be certain to write neatly. If the school can't read your phone number, for example, they can't call you if they have questions.

General Information

Read the schools' brochure, view book, and web site. What are the school's strengths? Which of the strengths are most important to you and your child? Work these into your application.

- But be honest. School personnel will know if you are pandering to them.
- Keep your answers simple and to the point (but fill up the allotted space). Don't digress. Try not to be wordy or long-winded. Don't use big words unless that's the way you normally speak. Above all, be yourself.

Describe Your Child's Strengths

All children have strengths. Describe your child's greatest strengths. Think about which of your child's strengths best complement the school's strengths. These are the areas you want to emphasize. For example, if the school is a creative, noncompetitive school, emphasize your child's creative abilities. (You needn't mention her competitive side.) If a school teaches languages at a very young age, perhaps you'll want to mention your child's facility with language.

Many applications will also ask you for your child's weaknesses. I would either ignore this question altogether or describe a quality that is common to many kids of your child's age. Some areas that you and your child might be working to improve, include

- learning to be more patient
- improving socialization skills
- learning to be more diplomatic when making a request
- remembering one's manners when excited
- learning to not ignore requests from parents

Don't list terrible negatives. That's what the student visit is for. Let the school ascertain whether your child has behaviors that will make him or her a poor fit for the school. Don't volunteer information here. And remember, what you perceive as a big deficiency or character flaw may, in reality, be typical behavior for a child of that age.

My Story: *I put this anecdote in one application to show my three-year-old daughter's creativity and quickness to understand new concepts:*

The other day, I was reading my daughter a story, and she began asking me questions—not about the story but about the structure of stories in general. I explained to her that a story has a problem, which the people in the story try to fix. That evening in the car, she made up a story that went something like this: Once upon a time, there were two girls named Day and Drop. Day had a problem. She wanted to fly, but she didn't know how. So she climbed a tree and flapped her arms, but she didn't have wings and she couldn't fly. So then Drop climbed the tree and said, "Why don't we hop onto an airplane?" So they hopped onto an airplane and flew home.

I was impressed because not only did my daughter create an original story with a problem but she also figured out a way to solve the problem and end the story.

Use Anecdotes

Using an anecdote is an effective way to show personality traits. If I said, "My daughter is creative and a fast learner," it would not have the same impact as showing these traits by describing something creative that my daughter actually did.

Essay Questions

The application may ask you to answer some essay-type questions, such as

- What are your (the parents') hobbies and interests?
- How does your child spend after-school time?
- What group activities does your child participate in?
- How much time each day does each parent spend with the child?
- What family activities does your child like?
- What type of discipline do you use?
- What are your child's responsibilities at home?
- What else do you want us to know about your child? Please attach an additional page if you want to tell us anything else that may be helpful to the Admissions Committee.

Let's address these questions one by one.

What are your (the parents') hobbies and interests? This is easy. Be truthful. Think about things you do that might seem like good qualities to the Admissions Committee. Are you involved in local politics or other activities in your community? Are you a coach? A member of your church? Active in your PTA? If you are, say so. These types of activities indicate that you are likely to become involved in the private school community to which your child is applying (and parent participation in school activities is important at private schools).

Now list your other hobbies and interests (these show you are a well-rounded, healthy individual). It probably doesn't matter whether you prefer sailing or fishing, camping or ballroom dancing. You are trying to paint an accurate picture of yourself. So describe yourself (and your spouse) as you are. Be proud of your interests. Don't try to portray yourself as someone you are not.

How does your child spend after-school time? Again, you want the school to get a feel for what your child is like. Describe your child's interests accurately, but be specific. Instead of saying, *she likes to play with her toys*, say something like *she creates elaborate birthday parties for her stuffed Dalmatians*.

What group activities does your child participate in? The purpose of this question is to get a good sense of your child and his interests. It also shows that your child can get along in a group. If your child is very young, he may not have been involved in many group activities, so you may want to mention group activities at parks or playgrounds, such as a weekly neighborhood potluck or a regular Tuesday play date, and so on.

Being involved in many activities shows a gregarious (or perhaps overscheduled?) child. Do not worry if your child doesn't have a group activity for every day of the week. Listing one or two activities is fine. If your child participates in many activities, list the ones he or she likes the best or is most committed to. Listing too many activities and clubs may make the admissions committee wonder if your child will have enough time to complete school work.

How much time each day does each parent spend with the child? Again, be honest. If you are a stay-at-home mom and spend much time each day with your child, then say so. Describe what you and your child do together. If you go to parks, farms, zoos, museums, beaches, then this is what you should mention.

If you work, that's okay, too. Describe activities you and your child enjoy each day. If you talk, sing, eat together, and read bedtime stories daily, then this is what you should mention. You want to show a nurturing home environment, but you don't have to be a superparent.

What family activities does your child like? Describe in a sentence or two things you do as a family on weekends, vacations, or free time. If you are a divorced or single parent, describe what you and your child do together. If you want the school to know that your child is part of a large and loving network, you may want to mention activities that involve grandparents, cousins, uncles, or aunts. Whether your family is large or small, nuclear or extended, describe what you do and enjoy. Admissions committees look for diversity, so don't feel that your family must conform to any one mold.

What type of discipline do you use? Answers can be brief. Avoid mention of negative forms of discipline, such as spanking, slapping, or yelling. However, children need limits and rules, so forms of discipline that involve setting limits and enforcing them fairly are fine. Using positive reinforcement to encourage good behaviors while ignoring bad behaviors is also acceptable. To answer this question honestly, think about how you typically respond when your child does something wrong. Then briefly describe (in one or two sentences) what you do.

What are your child's responsibilities at home? List as many age-appropriate responsibilities as will fit in the space. If you have more than will fit in the space, choose the ones that are the most typical or the ones that show the most maturity. If your child has a responsibility that is unusual or difficult, list it first.

Responsibilities young children may perform: putting away toys, setting the table, brushing teeth, combing hair, hand and face washing, hanging up coats, putting away shoes, putting dirty clothes in hamper.

Responsibilities older children may perform: washing dishes, taking out the trash, being a mother's helper, making lunches, shoveling snow, doing laundry, raking leaves, vacuuming.

Responsibilities teens may perform: baby-sitting, lawn mowing, painting, house cleaning, dog walking, grocery shopping, running errands, cooking meals.

What else do you want us to know about your child? Attach an additional page. Although the application may say this is optional, it is not. This is your opportunity to show your child's personality and strengths. Using a word processor, write a page describing your child's personality. Use anecdotes and examples. If your child is curious, SHOW how your child is curious. If your child is smart, SHOW how your child is smart. If your child is friendly or outgoing or mechanical or artistic,

SHOW what your child does that is friendly or outgoing or mechanical or artistic. Examples mean more than flowery words. People can get a picture of your child if they can visualize him or her doing something specific. You get the idea. Paint a picture of your child by using examples from real life.

Make your essays sound as if they are written just for this one application (even if you are using them in several applications). Work the name of the school into your essay; for example, you may want to end with something like *We would love to enroll Mikey in a school like the Willow School where we believe his boundless enthusiasm and curiosity would be welcomed, valued, and nurtured.*

Can I Supply More Than Is Asked For?

If an application doesn't say anything about attaching an additional page describing your child, you have several options:

- You can include the description anyway.
- You can call the school to see if it would be okay to attach a description. If it is, be sure to mention in your description who told you it was okay. Example: *Per my discussion with (Name) on (date), I am attaching the following description of my child to help you get to know her better.*

Be careful about supplying much more than the school requires. Admissions personnel may think that if you refuse to follow directions on a simple application, you may be difficult to deal with as a member of the school community.

My Story: *To show my daughter's sense of letter/sound correspondence (as well as her tender nature), I included an anecdote like this on several applications:*

My three-year-old daughter "writes" sentences with magnetic letters on the refrigerator. Last summer, I was outside getting groceries from the car, when she came running out to me with a magnetic *L* and a *V*. She said, "I'm writing *I love my Blacky* on the refrigerator. What other letters do I need to spell *love?*"

The Photograph

Many applications will ask you to attach an optional photograph of your child. Again, you should not think of this as being optional. It's important. A good photograph can reinforce what you've already written about your child in the application. It can show your child's personality. If you have a choice between attaching that professional photo you sent to all your relatives at Christmas and an unposed photo that captures your child's essence, I'd go with the latter.

If you have a photo that is engaging and will make the admissions personnel pause (or chuckle or sigh), this is the photo you want to attach. A smiling, generic photo beside a Christmas tree or fireplace is not as good as one that shows your child's personality, even if the lighting is better in the professional photograph.

Since schools strive for diversity, but they don't ask on the application for information about race, ethnicity, or religion, a carefully chosen photograph can supply the admissions committee with this needed information. If your child is not Caucasian, it is especially important to include a photograph. If the photograph shows something about your child's religious background, this may be useful information, too.

My Story: *After describing my daughter as a child who adores animals and who enjoys creating fantasies involving animals, I included in one application a photo of my daughter holding a giant pine cone and some straw. On the back of the photo, I wrote, "Momma duck with egg and nest." For this is exactly what my daughter was pretending to be—a momma duck with* *an egg and a nest. I felt this photograph reinforced the written description of my daughter that I had supplied earlier in the application.*

Teacher Recommendations

Most schools want teacher recommendations. Depending on the age of your child, you will be asked for different types of recommendations. Even students who are applying to prekindergarten, kindergarten, and first grade usually need to supply a school report from a school teacher, preschool teacher, or even a day-care provider. If your child is very young and has never been to any kind of school before, the school report can usually be waived.

Prekindergarten, Kindergarten, and First Grade For young children, the teacher is usually asked to write a brief appraisal of the child (a few lines long). The rest of the report is a checklist on which the teacher marks whether the child exhibits strength, is age appropriate, or needs development in many areas (such as, *playing alone, cooperating, sharing, following directions, listening, speech, curiosity, coordination, problem-solving abilities*). For first graders, the teacher may also be required to briefly describe the child's beginning literacy and math skills.

Grades Two, Three, and Four For students entering these grades, the school report is similar, but it also includes space for the teacher to describe a child's progress in academic subjects (reading, spelling, math, social studies, foreign language, writing, and so on). It asks for results of any achievement or IQ tests the student has taken. It may also ask the teacher to describe the child's special abilities, greatest strengths, if he is working up to capacity or has had special tutoring, and how active the parents are in the school community.

Grades Five and Higher The application process gets more complicated the older a child gets. Students in grades five and up are usually required to submit a school report similar to the one second through fourth graders submit. In addition, they may need a report from an English or language arts teacher AND a math teacher.

You can use a worksheet like the following to keep track of teacher recommendations.

Teacher Recommendations Worksheet

Math Teacher Name:

Recommendations Needed at	Date Due	Date Sent
School I:		
School 2:		
School 3:		
School 4:		
School 5:		
School 6:		

English/Language Arts Teacher Name:

Recommendations Needed at	Date Due	Date Sent
School I:		
School 2:		
School 3:		
School 4:		
School 5:		
School 6:		

Personal References

Many schools (even elementary schools) require one or two personal references. Some people feel that it is important to obtain references from parents who are already a part of the school community. Others feel it is important to get references from powerful people in the community who can write an impressive recommendation on fancy letterhead.

I think neither of these considerations is of utmost importance. The most important things you should worry about are finding someone who knows your child well and who can express themselves well in writing. After all, if the person says wonderful things about your child but produces a letter that is riddled with grammatical mistakes and misspellings, it may not help your cause. So find someone

- who can write well, and
- who knows your child's best qualities.

Letters of recommendation should be typed on one page. If the writer can't fit everything on one page, he or she should consider paring the text. The writer needs only to describe the child's most important qualities, not every aspect of her personality. Again, anecdotes or stories that illustrate the child's best qualities are always helpful.

You can use a worksheet like following to keep track of deadlines for personal references.

Personal References Worksheet

School 1   **Date Due**   **Date Completed**

Contact:
Phone Number:
Title:
School:
Address:
Address:
Notes:

School 2   **Date Due**   **Date Completed**

Contact:
Phone Number:
Title:
School:
Address:
Address:
Notes:

Letters of recommendation NOT needed for the following schools:

Student Questionnaires

Students in lower grades are not usually required to provide a writing sample or to answer written questions. However, children entering grade six and above will likely have to fill out a student questionnaire. The questionnaire may ask questions like

- What subjects do you like most and why?
- What musical or artistic activities do you enjoy?
- What sports do you play?
- What books have you read recently, and why did you like them?
- Who influenced you the most?
- Who do you most admire?
- What are you like as a person?

It's important for a student to think carefully about these answers because these questions may come up again during the school visit or interview.

Admissions Tests

Many applicants to grade six and higher must also take an admissions test—either the Secondary School Admissions Test (SSAT) or the Independent School Entrance Examination (ISEE). The school can provide registration forms for these tests, which usually need to be completed by January.

The SSAT

This test contains multiple-choice questions that measure math and verbal abilities. In addition, it includes a writing sample. The test takes more than two hours to finish. There are separate exams for students in grades five to seven and grades eight to eleven. The tests are given on Saturdays at more than 600 sites around the nation. Because each test is different, students can take the test many times. For more information, visit http://www.ssat.org, where you can request a free SSAT student guide and a sample test booklet.

The ISEE

This test contains multiple-choice questions that measure math and verbal abilities. In addition, there is a thirty-minute essay. The essay is not scored, but it gives schools a chance to see a student's writing ability. The test takes about three hours to finish. There are three separate exams, one for students applying to grades five and six, one for students applying to grades seven and eight, and one for students applying to grades nine through twelve. For more information, please visit http://www.erbtest.org, where you can request a free student guide and a sample test booklet that contains an actual practice test.

The Completed Application

When the application is completed and you are satisfied with it, make a copy and send it to the school by regular mail with a check to cover the application fee (usually $30 to $50). If you want to be certain the application was received, you can have the Post Office send you a notice indicating the application has been delivered. Many schools will send you a postcard acknowledging the receipt of your application. If you haven't heard from a school in a couple of weeks, you can make a brief, polite call to the school to confirm that the application has arrived.

When you think that all of the many components of your application have been completed and mailed, you should call to confirm that your application package is now complete. (Once in a while, a school doesn't want you to call, but school personnel will generally let you know this during one of your visits. Most schools are happy to double-check your application folder and to answer your questions about whether or not your application is complete. If a school does not want you to contact them regarding the completed application, I think I would seriously reconsider whether or not I want to send my child to a school that dislikes sincere questions from earnest parents.)

Chapter 7
January: The Child Visit and Financial Aid

Most schools want to see the child before the admissions decisions are made. If the child is very young, he or she will usually be expected to come in for an hour or two to play. This might be in a small group of only one or two children, or it might be in a much larger group of up to fifteen children. During this time, a teacher or admissions person may ask the child some questions. These questions usually are intended to assess a child's literacy, math, and verbal skills. There may be questions about letter/sound correspondence, counting, shapes, or colors. Older children likely will be asked slightly harder questions on the same topics.

School personnel also want to see whether your child is energetic or calm, outgoing or quiet, obedient or challenging, and so on. Since schools like to have classrooms in which there is a mix of personality types, don't worry about your child's personality. The school is looking for some children who are just like yours.

What to Expect

Think about what is best for your young child before you schedule a visit. Are the visits scheduled from October to January? If so, think about your child's needs. Visits in October probably have fewer children and may be easier for your child to handle. However, if your child is just beginning preschool and you would like your child to gain a little more assurance about being in a school setting or separating from you, then you might want to schedule your visit for January. After all, your child is older in January, and a few months might make a big difference in his or her readiness, especially if your child is very young.

It is probably best not to make a big deal out of the visit. Prepare young children by telling them they are going to a school to have a play date. At the school, the child will meet new friends and play with toys. Encourage the child to be polite, but do not put pressure on your child to perform for this is likely to backfire. Cross your fingers, and hope for the very best. The teachers your child will meet are experienced with and enjoy young children. You child will probably have a very good time, impress the teachers, and leave with a smile on her face.

The parents are generally herded into a separate room nearby, where they can ask questions of school personnel or listen to a talk about the school. This is a good opportunity for parents to talk to administrators and other parents. Before you attend this session, think about what you really want to find out about this school, and then ask.

Schools generally realize that separating from parents is hard for some young children, and they will try to make the process easier. Most are experienced at keeping young children engaged and happy. However, if the process is difficult for your child and the teachers seem rigid in their attitudes, you may want to think about how much your child will enjoy the school.

Children in upper elementary, middle school, and high school, will often be expected to visit for an entire school day. Sometimes they will be chaperoned by school personnel who will show your child the classrooms and activities that she is most interested in. At other schools, the student may be paired with another student in his or her grade who will show your child around the school for the day. This may be an exciting experience for your child, but it can also be intimidating and stressful.

You can help calm your child's nerves by preparing, before the visit, a checklist of things to evaluate while at the school. Making the list will help your child think about what is important to him about a school. Students may want to rank (from 1 to 10) the classrooms, cafeteria, playing fields, athletic facilities, computer labs, music classes, art classrooms, language classrooms, or whatever is of special interest. They may also want to assess whether or not the other kids seem friendly, smart, happy, bored, hard working, poised, and so on, and whether the teachers seem friendly, easy, hard, caring, approachable. Students may also want to think about the work, the classes, the extracurricular activities, the best things about the school, the worst things about the school. Your child can write these questions on a sheet of paper and make notes as the school visit progresses.

Your child will probably be asked some questions, and may even have a formal interview. Students should be reminded to sit up straight and to look the interviewer in the eye during an interview. Before the visit, practice shaking hands using a firm grip, if necessary. Make sure students are well groomed and dressed more-or-less like the others at the school. (This will make the student fit in better, and he will be less self-conscious about the visit.) If the school has a uniform, have your child dress in clothes that are similar (for example, khaki pants and a dark polo shirt). If the school does not have a dress code, observe what children wear. If they are all wearing blue jeans, then it is acceptable for your child to dress that way. If they are all wearing ties or dresses, then your child should wear a tie or a dress.

Prepare your child for the interview by reviewing the questions on the application. If your child is amenable, you can practice interviewing. If your child doesn't want to practice, encourage him to think about how he will respond to the questions.

Many interviewers begin by reviewing the application with the student. They are trying to get a sense of the child, and they are also trying to put the child at ease, so he can give well-thought out responses. Interviewers don't expect children to have the analytical or verbal skills of an adult, so whatever your child says is probably fine.

The interview may ask questions, such as
- What do you like best about school?
- What is your favorite subject?
- What makes a class enjoyable to you?
- What activities do you like outside the classroom?
- What are your favorite books, movies, or games? Why?
- What do you do in your spare time?
- Whom do you admire, and why?
- What can you contribute to this school?
- What are your plans after you graduate?
- If you could change anything in the world, what would it be?

Encourage your child to make a list of questions he or she would like to ask the interviewer about the school, the students, the teachers, the curriculum, special activities, and so on. Having such a list prepared will reassure the student that she has something to fall back on if she needs something to say.

Most visits and interviews go very well. But if your child had a bad experience or was not feeling well, let the school know. The school might be able to set up another visit and interview at a later date.

You may want to use a worksheet like the following to keep track of when your child is scheduled to visit schools.

Student Visit Worksheet

School   **Date**   **Time**

School 1:

School 2:

School 3:

School 4:

School 5:

School 6:

No visit required at

Is This a Parent Interview, Too?

Yes. Oh, they may not call it an interview. They may just invite you to chat or visit while your child is busy, but make no doubt about it, the school administrators care about what you have to say. And what you say can have a big influence on whether or not your child is accepted.

If you are in a large group of other parents, you may not have a chance to contribute much. But if you are the only parent, or if there are only one or two others, then what you say is important. You may want to discuss three things: how much you like the school, what your child is like, or what you can contribute to the school. Administrators love to hear your thoughts in all of these areas. Remember, schools like diversity and individuality. Try not to say what you think everyone else is saying. Think about how you and your child can contribute to the school in a unique way that will enhance the school community. Share your thoughts.

In addition, you are also assessing the school faculty and administrators. Notice how they behave. Do they seem passionate and enthusiastic? Do they love talking about their students? Are they excited by the curriculum? These are all good signs.

Applying for Financial Aid

Private schools can cost a small fortune. You may think, because of the price tag, that such schools are out of your reach. But you might be wrong. Most schools offer financial aid. About 20 percent of students in private schools receive some form of financial aid.

The financial aid process is pretty much the same at most independent schools. First, you must fill out and send in the Parents' Financial Statement (PFS) to the School and Student Service (SSS) for Financial Aid in Princeton, New Jersey. On this form, you list all of the schools you are applying to. The

SSS will then send a letter to each of these schools telling them how much money they think you are able to pay toward tuition at the school. Schools are under no obligation to award you financial aid to make up the difference, but many will. They might even award you more than the SSS thinks you need.

The SSS analyzes your Parents' Financial Statement and decides how much you can afford to pay. This amount is the same whether you have one child in school or six children in school. So the cost of sending one child to private school or sending six children to private school would be the same. If, for example, the SSS thinks you can afford to pay $16,000 per year, you will be expected to pay this entire amount each year. If you have one child, the entire $16,000 will go to that child's tuition. But if you have two children in school, you will be expected to pay $8,000 per child. If you have four children in school, you will be expected to pay $4,000 per child.

Business/Farm Statement

If you are self-employed, you will need to complete a Business/Farm Statement before you complete the Parents' Financial Statement. Send a copy of this form to each school to which you are applying. These forms are usually due in January. Much of the information on these forms comes from Schedule C of your federal taxes, so you will either need to complete your federal taxes (which is virtually impossible in January) or estimate as accurately as possible (which is acceptable).

On page one of this form, you will be asked to list your business or farm income and expenses, gross profit, total business or farm income, wages, business property, business expenses, and total profit or loss. Page two requires you to list your business or farm assets and debts, such as land and buildings, cash reserves, livestock, debts, mortgage, and so on. Much of this information is found on either Schedule C,

Schedule F, or Form 1120, depending on the type of business you own.

A copy of this form is sent directly to the schools to which you are applying. Do not send this form back to the Educational Testing Service (ETS). They will not look at it.

The Parents' Financial Statement

The Parents' Financial Statement can be a daunting form. It is four pages long, and you will have to have your income taxes completed—or at least near completion—to fill out the form. Since many schools require this form to be completed in January, it can be difficult to pull all your tax information together in time to complete the form. You are allowed to estimate on some items, but you have to indicate on the form that you are estimating.

Part I: Student and Family Information

Part A asks for information about the student or students, birth dates, and who the child or children live with. Part B asks for information about the parents or guardians and the names of the schools that you want copies of the report sent to.

Part C asks for information about the parents taxable and nontaxable income as well as medical and dental expenses. Part D asks for information about family assets and debts, such as home ownership, bank accounts, investments, debts, student assets, and other real estate.

Part II: Supplemental Information

Part II asks questions such as how much you think you can afford to pay. (It doesn't seem to matter what you say here, however. The ETS's conclusion about how much you can afford doesn't seem to have anything to do with how you answer this question, as far as I can figure out.) The form also asks for the names of the schools your children attend; whether or not you have a retirement plan; childcare expenses; value of life insurance policies; club dues; costs of camps and lessons; costs of vacations; values of cars and other vehicles owned; and so on.

If parents are separated, divorced, or have never been married, they are required to fill out a special section in Part II. Last, parents need to provide brief, written explanations for all numbered items in the form with circles around them (if you did not answer zero to these items). These are items such as other taxable income, Social Security benefits, unusual expenses, bank accounts, investments, debts, stocks, business assets, unpaid principle on home mortgage, and so on.

Part III: Parent Certification

This is the easiest section. Here, they just want you to sign and date the form and provide home and work telephone numbers. Congratulations! You're done.

Copies of Financial Documents

Now you just have to make photocopies of the PFS (one for each school you are applying to and one for your records). Then write a check to the Educational Testing Service (ETS) and mail in your completed form. For a small additional fee, you can have a copy of the report sent to you directly. I would recommend this. The report will give you a sense of how much financial aid you are eligible for before you receive your acceptance letters.

You may think that the hardest part is over, and perhaps it is, but you still have to send to the schools to which you are applying copies of your W-2s, 1099s, and sometimes even your completed tax forms. Often these items are not due until after the acceptance letters have been mailed (usually in March), and your financial aid may be contingent upon receiving these documents.

But at other schools, you will need to send in copies of your filed tax forms by mid-February! If this is the case, you will be scrambling like a madman in January to compile all the necessary documentation, so you can have your taxes completed and filed by mid-February. This is truly a pain in the neck, but once you have your taxes filed early, you can smile in April when your friends talk about standing in hour-long lines to mail their taxes on April 15.

You may want to use a form like the following to keep track of the steps involved in the financial aid process.

Financial Aid Checklist

Name of School:
Phone Number/Contact Name:

Form	Date Due	Date Completed
❑ Parents' Financial Statement (PFS) to SSS in New Jersey		
❑ Copy of PFS to school		
❑ Preliminary financial aid application		
❑ Signed copy of IRS form 4506		
❑ Business/Farm Statement		
❑ Previous year's federal tax return and schedules and forms		
❑ Current federal tax return		
❑ W-2s and 1099s		
❑ School Scholarship form		
❑ After-school worksheet		
❑ Additional information		

Chapter 8
February: The Waiting Game

By the time February rolls around, you are pretty much done with the application process. Oh, you may still have one or two loose ends to tie up, you might have a child visit scheduled, or a W-2 to send in, but for the most part, you are done. Doesn't it feel good? Probably yes and no.

You're glad to be finished with all the work that applying entails, but you are also anxious to hear if your child has been accepted. Many schools notify applicants in March about whether or not they are accepted, so now you have to cool your heels for a month or so.

Hurry Up and Wait!

One thing you may want to do now is to rank your choices. When decision letters are mailed out in March, you will not have much time to make a decision, so it's a good idea to start thinking now about which schools are your favorites.

If you child is old enough, you child should rank the schools, too. Then both parents and child can compare rankings. If you are lucky, you will both agree on your favorite schools. But what should you do if you don't?

First, find out why your child has ranked the schools the way he or she has. If she is afraid that one school is too hard or too competitive, you may want to work on alleviating her fears. But if she likes the atmosphere, the teachers, or the students at a particular school, you may have a hard time changing her mind about her ranking. Don't make a big issue out of it—at least not yet. She hasn't been accepted yet anyway.

Explain why you like your favorites, and let her think about your reasoning for a while. She may agree with you over time, or she may not. If she doesn't, there's not much you can do about it. If you are like most people, the more you learn about a school, the more you like it. You may realize that your child's preferred schools are pretty good schools.

Early Acceptance Letters

It's possible you will get an acceptance letter early. Sometimes schools want to get you to commit to them before offers from more competitive schools arrive. If this happens, consider yourself lucky. But do not commit to a school until you have weighed all of your offers.

If you get an early acceptance letter, you may worry that if you don't accept the offer, you will find yourself in a month with a stack of rejection letters from other schools and no place to go. It's a valid fear, but do your best to allow yourself to consider all of your options.

Oftentimes, early acceptance letters are mailed about one month before decision letters at other schools are mailed. After you receive all of your decision letters (including the one that was mailed a month early), you may still have a couple of days before you have to respond to the school that mailed you the early decision letter. If this is the case, be prepared to act quickly. Plan what you are going to do when the other decision letters arrive.

If you get into a school you prefer more, contact the early acceptance school immediately. A written letter is best, but if time is short, call the school. Tell them you are sorry but you have decided not to accept their wonderful offer.

The decision becomes muddier if you find out you are wait-listed at a preferred school. You need to respond to the early decision school right away. You can't wait long enough to find out if you are accepted into your preferred school.

You might consider calling the school and asking if you can have a short extension to decide. Tell them the truth, that you have applied to other schools, too, and you'd like to weigh all options before making a decision. They may or may not give you an extension.

If they don't, consider sending in the money to hold your child's place at the school. You may have to forfeit the money later if you go with a better school, but you are between a rock and a hard place. Paying the money will give you some time. But it won't give you an indefinite amount of time. Most contracts state that if you don't cancel within thirty days, you are liable for the full amount of the year's tuition whether your child attends the school or not. Ouch! So make sure you read the contract carefully before signing it and sending it in. Know what you have to do and by when. Mark important decision dates on your calendar.

Chapter 9
March: Letters Good and Bad

If you've applied to competitive schools, the odds of receiving a rejection letter are high. These schools have many, many applicants for only a few openings. Don't let a rejection letter disappoint you too much, and if your child has her heart set on a school that rejected her, explain that even if one's qualifications are outstanding, there is just not enough room at the school for all qualified applicants. Explain to your child, too, that schools try for balance. For example, if there are ten spaces available, five of the spaces will go to boys and five to girls. If twenty girls and six boys apply for the openings, then each boy has a much better chance of being accepted than each girl. Sometimes, that's just the way it works.

Explain to your child that being accepted is a numbers game. Your child is not being rejected because of skills, intelligence, or abilities. Your child is being rejected because the school doesn't have enough spaces for all qualified applicants.

Wait Listing

Being told that you are wait-listed is perhaps the most difficult news to receive because your options are not clear. Being wait-listed means that your child is qualified for the school, and that the school believes your child would be a good fit at the school, but that there are not enough spaces available at the moment. If a slot does open up, your child might be admitted to the school. But a slot might not open up, and even if it does, your child still might not be admitted. You just do not know.

So how do you know what your chances are if you are wait-listed? Well, if the school is one that your child really wants to attend, call the school. Ask them what the chances of being accepted are. Sometimes schools will tell you where on the waiting list your child is (say number 1 or number 2) and that your odds of getting in are good. Other times where a child is on the waiting list doesn't really matter. The school selects a student from the waiting list who best matches up with a student who has been accepted but decided not to attend the school. For example, if a boy has been accepted but decides not to attend, the school will likely choose another boy from the waiting list rather than a girl.

If you decide that you will attend a public school if you don't get in to the private school at which you are wait-listed, you are in pretty good shape. There are no contracts with other schools to sign, so you are free to attend the private school if a space opens up—even if the space doesn't become available until late August.

But if you sign a contract with another school, and you adjust to the idea of going to this school (and, in fact, are even looking forward to this school), it's probably best to call the school at which your child has been wait-listed and tell them to remove your child's name from the list.

What if a school at which you are wait-listed calls you in August to tell you they have an opening for your child, but you have already signed a contract and paid tuition at another school? You will have to decide how much you want to get into the school that wait-listed you. You probably cannot get out of your contract with the other school, so you are faced with the dilemma of having to pay two sets of tuition if you want to go to the school at which your child is wait-listed. Most people would probably not want to do this, but if money is not an issue or admittance at this school is supremely important, then this is certainly an option.

Acceptance Letters

If you receive more than one acceptance letter, you will have to decide (rather quickly) which school your child will attend. The financial aid offers you receive may help drive your decision.

Comparing Financial Aid Offers

If you are choosing between two similar schools but one offers you a much better financial aid package, the choice is easy. Some schools have more financial aid to distribute, and so they may offer you a much better package than a school without much financial aid to distribute.

Some parents decide that going to the best school (no matter the cost) will help their child get scholarships to good colleges. They may decide, in the end, that sacrificing now will mean they have fewer college bills later. However, if your child is very young, this is something of a gamble. You don't really know what the college-admissions process will be like in fifteen years. If your child is entering a private high school, however, this may be an easier decision to make.

Comparing Schools

Many schools have events (receptions, lectures, parties, play dates, performances) for students who have been accepted into the school but have not yet reached a decision about whether or not to attend the school. This is another chance to visit the school and talk to teachers, parents, and students about the school. Think about what you really need to know to make a decision about whether or not to attend this school. What questions do you still have about this school? Attend the event with your questions in mind.

In addition to prepared events, you may want to pay a second visit to each of the schools at which your child has been accepted. Sometimes seeing a school in action is a more helpful indicator of what a school is like than attending a preplanned event. Perhaps it's been so long since you visited that you cannot remember the layout or the facilities or even what the teachers are like. Now is the time to refresh your memory and notice the small details.

Dust off those checklists that you made earlier in the year. Now that you and your child have visited many schools, you may have a better sense of what you want to know about the schools you are deciding between. You may want to ask for names of current parents with whom you can discuss the school.

If your child is very smart, find out if the school will challenge your student enough. How flexible are the groupings? For example, if a second grader is working at a sixth-grade level in math, what does the school do? If a prekindergarten student has taught herself to read, how will the school handle it? If your child wants to take fifth-year Spanish, will that be possible? If you child needs special support, which school will best meet your child's individual needs? Make sure your child understands what courses are offered and during what school years. Don't assume that every class listed in the catalog is offered every year.

Choosing a School

Once you have made a decision about which school to attend, you should contact all the other schools at which you were accepted to let them know your decision. It's fastest to call on the phone, but you might prefer to compose a polite letter explaining (briefly) your decision.

Sometimes you can eliminate one school before you have made your final decision about which school to attend. Contact the school you have eliminated as soon as you decide. This will make it easier for the school to offer your child's space to another student in a timely fashion.

Chapter 10
April: Your Decision Is Made (Finally!)

The decision deadline arrives. You have made your decision. You sign a contract and send in a large chunk of money. Now you can relax, right? Perhaps. But there are other decisions to be made.

To Attend Summer Camp or Not?

After you are accepted at a school, you often have the option of attending summer camp at the school. This can be a good opportunity for your child to meet classmates and teachers. It can also be a chance for you to meet other parents, neighbors, and teachers, too. Summer camp is discussed in greater detail in chapter 13, but if you are making the decision now, I suggest you skip ahead to find questions to ask while you are evaluating summer programs.

Declining Other Offers

Many people call on the telephone to decline offers. This is swift and efficient, but I feel it is a little more polite to write a pleasant note detailing some of the good qualities of the school. You should also explain how difficult the decision was for you, but that you have decided to attend another school.

Attend School Picnics, Fairs, or Other Get-Togethers

Before the school year ends, many schools schedule a picnic, fair, party, or other get-togethers so that new families to the school can meet families who already have students at the school. This is a good opportunity to meet nearby neighbors who attend your school (and, in fact, your neighbors may have already been told about you and will seek you out at the event). You may also be able to meet children who will be in your child's class, parents and teachers, coaches and instructors, and many other people affiliated with the school.

Take this opportunity to walk around the school grounds and familiarize your child with the location of the playground, pool, playing fields, tennis or basketball courts, and so on. If your child is like most, he or she will begin to look forward to the day in September when he or she can start going to this new and exciting school.

Chapter 11
May: The New School

In May, the new school to which your child has been accepted may send many forms for you to fill out, including emergency contact forms and health forms. It is important to fill out and return these forms quickly because many other forms will soon be on their way to your home, and it is best not to get behind already.

Health Forms

Health forms need to be completed by a physician, so you may need to make a doctor's appointment for your child if he or she has not had a physical examination recently. The health forms are important to complete in a timely fashion, for if the school does not receive them on time, your child may not be able to enter the school in September. And remember, it can take several months to schedule a doctor's visit at this time of year, for many children need to get checkups to enter school or to participate in sports or summer activities. So schedule any needed appointments right away, or you may find yourself panicking in July or August.

What to Do If You Did Not Get In

Many schools have only a few openings each year. Most applicants do not get in. If you did not get in to the school you wanted, or if you are new to a town and would like to find a good school for the fall, it is not too late to start looking. The most competitive schools are probably already filled, but there are still plenty of other good schools around that are looking for students to fill out their classroom rosters.

It's Never Too Late to Apply

Many good schools are still accepting new students throughout the summer. Some parents and students don't realize until late in a school year that they want or need a change. Don't worry. There is hope. You still have time to find a school that will meet your child's needs.

The down side of applying to a school in the spring or summer, however, is that there will be no financial aid available. By this time of year, the aid has all been distributed. You may be eligible for aid the following year, but you are out of luck for the upcoming school year.

Rolling Admissions

The admissions time frame will be compressed if you apply in the spring or summer. You will have to work fast. You will have to quickly learn about each school, make visits, and decide to which school or schools you want to apply to. Learn from your past mistakes. If you applied to so many schools in the fall that you didn't have time to do a good job on the applications and essays, slow down. Take your time. Apply to only one or two schools. Since time is short, you don't want to try to do too much.

Contact Schools

Before you start visiting schools, you may want to winnow your choices by calling the schools and collecting some information. Be honest with the schools. Tell them about your child's academic and social abilities. Find out if the admissions officer thinks your student is a good fit for their school. You will often be able to get a good sense during this telephone interview about whether your child is likely to get into the school or not. If it sounds unlikely, you probably will not want to waste time applying. If your student does not seem like a good fit, ask for the names of schools at which your child might be a good candidate and call these schools.

After making calls to schools in the area, you may have a very good sense of which schools your child is likely to be able to get into. You may feel good because you know there are openings available, and the school representative encourages you to apply. Keep the lines of communication open during the summer. Call the representative every couple of weeks to see if your application is moving along and if the picture still looks rosy. Many parents of students applying in the spring or summer have a good sense that their child will get in to the school long before acceptance letters are mailed.

Chapter 12
June: Summer Reading Lists (and More)

In June, the new school is liable to send you or your student summer reading lists and summer work packets. It is important for your child to get copies of the recommended books and to actually read them. In addition, he or she should seriously apply him- or herself to the work in the packets. The new school may be more academically rigorous than the school he or she is used to, but now is the time to get used to the discipline it takes to keep up. If your child completes the assigned work, he or she can feel confident when entering the school on the first day. If the work has not been completed, the first days of the new school year will be filled with anxiety and dread rather than excitement.

In addition, the new school may send in June extended-day enrollment forms or important information about the after-school program. Students may also have to schedule a meeting with foreign language teachers to ascertain their level of foreign language proficiency.

Rolling Admissions: Keep Trying

If you are applying to a school now, you should have narrowed your choices by June. Now you will have to complete the same steps that you completed earlier in the year—only in less time. These include

- the parent interview
- the application
- letters of recommendation
- child essays, test scores, grades, report cards
- a child visit

The Interview

The school will likely want to know why you are applying late. Be truthful. If you applied to a very competitive school but didn't get in, you have nothing to hide. Most other applicants did not get in to this school either. If you decide late in the year that your child's current school is not a good fit, explain why you came to this realization and what you are looking for in a school. If you have just moved to the area, let the school administrators know.

Student Data

Collect and organize students data, such as test scores, report cards, writing samples, and so on. You will want to get this information into the hands of the school admissions personnel as soon as possible, so they can make a quick decision.

Academic Performance

If you child's academic performance is weak in one area, you may want to enroll her in a summer program to bolster her skills in this area. If you plan to do so, tell the school to which you are applying. This may strengthen your candidacy. At the very least, it will show the school that you are serious about being able to meet their academic standards and that you will help your child as needed.

The Application

Complete the applications. You may be able to use some of the information on applications you submitted to other schools as a guideline, but before you do, examine each one carefully.

- Are you presenting an accurate picture of your student?
- Is there other information that would be useful?
- Have you neglected to say anything that might enhance your child's chance of acceptance.

You might want to show your application to another person who knows your child well.

- Are you showcasing your child's best qualities?
- Does the child in the application sound like your child?

Think carefully about why your earlier applications were not successful.

- Is there any way that you can improve on what you have written before?
- Has your child grown or changed since the fall?
- What are his new interests?

Certainly, you will be able to write about more recent activities and experiences. Perhaps your child has matured immensely since the beginning of the year. If this is the case, be certain to mention this both in the application and at the interview.

Follow-up Calls

Because time is short, you will want to make follow-up calls to ascertain that applications have been received and that all required documents are in place. You may be able to get a sense of what your child's chances of acceptance are. Don't push the issue if the admissions officer does not want to discuss it, but often families find that they feel confident at this point about their chances of admittance.

Chapter 13
July: Summer Camp

In July, the new school may send you some or all of the following: a school information letter, a transportation form (to figure out how your child will be getting to and from the school), a carpool list by town, a bus transportation form, a brochure about special programs, and an after-school program enrollment form. Again, fill out the appropriate forms and return them to the school as quickly as possible.

Summer Camp

Once you have chosen a school, you may have the option of sending your child to a summer program at the school. This can be a good opportunity for your child to meet some classmates and make some friends in an informal setting. This can also be a good opportunity for you to meet other parents, discuss carpooling, and find out about the culture and traditions of the school.

In addition, a good summer program can provide valuable opportunities for your child to get plenty of exercise, explore unfamiliar activities, and learn new things about himself. Some programs are day programs while others are overnight programs. Depending on the age and personality of your child, you may want to choose either option.

Before you sign your child up, however, you may want to ask a few questions, such as

- What do you do if a child doesn't want to participate in an activity?
- How do you resolve conflicts?
- What if my child doesn't like sports? or crafts?
- What do children learn and do? How are they sorted? by age? size? skill level?

- What is unique about this program?
- How long is the program? All day? every day? mornings?
  one week? two weeks? all summer?
- Are leadership skills nurtured?
- What is the ratio of staffers to children?
- How old are the staffers? What experience do they have?
  How are staffers trained?

If you have the opportunity to talk to other parents about the
program, you may want to ask the following:
- How did your child like the program?
- What was the child's favorite part of the program? least
  favorite part?
- How did your child like the staff?
- How did you as a parent like the program? What did
  you dislike?

Finally, you will want to ask yourself these questions:
- Is the camp a good fit for my child? Why?
- Will the structure suit my child?
- Will the size suit my child?

Meet Teachers, Classmates, and Parents

Once you have decided to attend summer camp, your child may
find it a good time to make some friends before the school year
starts. It can also be an opportunity for you to meet other
parents and establish some contacts. You may find a friendly
parent who lives nearby. Perhaps now you feel relieved because
you have a backup driver if you are ill or need someone to
carpool with.

You can talk to other parents to find out about the culture
of the school.

- Do parents and kids get together socially after school, especially on early-release days?
- Do they meet somewhere?
- What about vacations and holidays?

You may be able to meet and establish a rapport with school administrators or some of your child's current or future teachers. This might come in useful in the future if a problem arises at the school. Establishing a relationship before there is a problem is a good idea. Now you have an ally at the school who knows you and your child and to whom you can turn for advice and help.

Chapter 14
August: Preparing for the New School

In August, the new school may send you some or all of the following: a map of the school, a letter from the head of the school, lists of students in each class, a parent handbook, a school calendar, information about the parents' association, information about clubs or athletic programs, and field trip information.

Prepare

August is a time of anticipation, perhaps anxiety, and hope. Your child knows he or she will soon be attending a new school. You can ease the transition by visiting the school (many schools have special activities for new students) and arranging some play dates or activities with other students at the school before school starts. You can call the school to see if they will give you the names of some students who live near you. If they can't give you this information, you can try to meet these parents and students at an activity arranged by the school.

Visit the School and Classroom

Your child may be able to use the school's playground, basketball or tennis courts, or other outdoor facilities during the summer. This is a good opportunity to get your child used to the drive to the school as well as an opportunity for your child to get used to the school grounds. You can walk around outside the school, pointing out the classrooms and the gym and other attractions. This will help your child feel more familiar with the school when school finally does start, usually in September.

If you have an opportunity to go inside the school, often during an orientation day for new students, it is time to look at specifics:

- Where is your child's classroom?
- Where is the bathroom? How do you get from the classroom to the bathroom and back?
- Where will the child put his or her things?
- Where will the child sit?
- Where is the lunchroom? How do you get from the classroom to the lunchroom and back? Do students typically bring a lunch or buy a lunch? If students bring a lunch, where do they keep it until lunchtime? Do students carry lunchboxes or brown-bag lunches?
- Who is the homeroom teacher? What is her name? Who are the other teachers?
- How many other children are in the classroom? Where do they sit?
- Where is the playground? You may be able to use the playground during the summer and to inspect the outside of the school.
- What supplies are needed on the first day?
- What kind of clothes do students at this school typically wear?

Buy Clothes and Supplies

August is also a time to buy school clothes and accessories; however, you may not want to buy too many items in advance. You may want to give your child a month or so to figure out what the other students wear and what he or she would like to wear. At some schools, students wear ties and skirts. At others, the dress is more casual. But there is a big difference between khaki pants and polo shirts and jeans and T-shirts. So don't make too many clothing purchases just yet. Give your child a chance to observe what others wear for a few weeks. (During the first week or two of school, students often dress more formally than they dress later on. So it is probably best to wait about a month before you make your clothing decisions.)

In addition, you child will want to observe backpacks and lunchboxes. After she has an idea of the style she wants, then you can make the purchase. But if you buy a backpack in August that is embarrassing by the end of September, you will feel as if you have wasted your money. So don't get too carried away by the excitement of going to a new school. Try to stay rational and patient. Make most of your purchases in late September when you can feel more confident about the long-term usefulness of what you are buying.

Chapter 15
Students with Special Needs

Often parents who have children with special needs will seek out a private school in which to educate their child. Since private schools often have lower student-teacher ratios, these parents believe that their child will get more individual attention and will have a better learning experience at a private school than at a public school.

While it is true that private schools are often small and intimate, it is especially important to find a school that is a good fit if your child has special needs, learning difficulties, or social or emotional problems that can make learning difficult.

Some schools are specifically designed to teach children with specific learning difficulties. If you have such a school near you, this may be one of the first places you will want to look to find a good fit for your child. A good resource for finding schools for children with all sorts of learning difficulties is http://www.schwablearning.org. At this site, you can find lists of schools by state to help you begin your search.

Specialized Schools

There are often many benefits to attending a school that specializes in specific learning difficulties. These schools can help students reach their potential by addressing their specific needs. At this type of school, students' self-esteem grows, for their strengths are enhanced and they receive remedial help with their weaknesses. Difficult concepts are often taught in ways that engage all of the senses. Each teacher has specialized training that allows him or her to provide the training that is most helpful to each individual student. The teachers at these schools understand and are sensitive to students who learn differently. These students' needs are met, and they are not unfairly labeled "lazy" or "stupid."

Specialized schools offer research-based instruction that can help a student make great academic strides. Furthermore, the students gain self-confidence, understand how they learn best, learn to advocate for themselves, recognize both their strengths and weaknesses, and often reach their potential for the first time.

It is important to visit a school to find out if it will suit your child. Methodologies at specialized schools vary greatly, and you want to find a school that is a good fit for your child. You may want to ask questions, such as the following:

- What remedial help does the school provide? How does it develop strengths?
- What populations does the school serve best? What levels of cognitive development; levels of reading, writing, and math skills; levels of social development; and types of behavior can the school address?
- What expectations does the school have for its students?
- What is the school's mission?
- How does the school measure student progress?
- What training do the teachers have? What programs are used?
- What technology is available? How is it used?
- How is the program individualized?

Mainstream Schools

But what if you don't have such a specialized school nearby, or what if you prefer your child attend a more mainstream school? How do you find a school that will be a good fit? You will have to do a lot of searching. Begin by visiting nearby schools. Ask lots of questions to try to ascertain whether or not the school would be a good fit for your child.

How do you explain your child's special needs to school personnel without harming your chances of being accepted into a school? This can be difficult, but I would suggest that during the preliminary stages, you not mention your child's learning difficulties. During school fairs or informal open houses, you can ask school administrators and teachers questions about how much they individualize instruction to meet the needs of students. You may want to ask what they do if a child is very advanced in a subject or if a child is falling behind in a subject. Based on the responses to these very broad questions, you will probably be able to figure out whether or not you want to pursue enrolling your child at a specific school.

One of the best places to ask many questions is during open houses. You have not yet applied to the school and are able to remain fairly anonymous. There will be many other parents there, so the staff at the school will probably not remember who asked what questions.

Try to ask questions of other parents or teaching specialists (such as music, art, shop, gym teachers). These teachers are unlikely to be involved in the admissions process, so you can ask them questions without worrying about hurting your chances for admissions at a later date.

Some questions that may be of special importance to you might be questions like these:

- What kinds of support or resources are available for my child and other children who may need them?
- Do you have a learning specialist at your school? What is this person's background and areas of expertise?
- What subjects are covered each year, and what ways can students approach these subjects? That is, are only books used, or is a variety of media used, including film, audiotapes, or online materials.

If your child has already been evaluated by a learning specialist, you may have insight into her learning styles or learning gaps. As you observe the school, keep your child's strengths and weaknesses in mind. Think carefully about how your child learns, and what environment will be best for him or her. Consider these questions:

- What are your child's strengths and weaknesses as a learner?
- What are her personality and social skills like?
- What are his interests?
- Does he like a structured or unstructured environment?
- Does she like large groups or individualized attention?
- What distracts from learning, such as noise, lights, crowds, and so on.
- Under what conditions does my child learn best?

Narrowing Your Choices

After you have narrowed your choices, then you will want to visit schools and ask more questions. It is important, at this point, to let the school know about your child's learning styles, needs, and gaps. Remember, you want to get your child into a school where he or she will thrive and grow. If the school does not have a complete picture of your child, it may not be able to meet his or her needs adequately, and your child may end up miserable and unhappy.

You will want to talk with school administrators and ask questions about the following:

- the school's approach to education
- its educational philosophy
- how students are evaluated
- how often standardized tests are taken
- how much time children spend on homework
- the schools approach to discipline
- opportunities for parents to become involved in the direction of the school and to act as advocates for their child
- the teaching methods used to reach out to every child

Be sure to observe classes with students in attendance. If the school has special education programs, ask to see them. Think about the following questions:

- Would your child be comfortable in the schools' classrooms and be able to learn?
- How are teachers reaching students who are having difficulties? For example, if a student is having trouble understanding a math concept, what do teachers do about it? Do they find other ways to approach the concept, such as using computers, manipulatives, pictures, tactile methods, aural methods, visual methods, and so on?
- Do teachers seem to bolster the students' self-esteem and confidence?
- Are they aware of different learning styles?
- Do they teach students themselves about different learning styles, so the students can learn to help themselves get the most out of every lesson, even after they no longer attend the school?

What Should I Expect After My Child Is Accepted?

Once your child is accepted, your responsibilities are not over. As a parent, you will want to advocate for your child in school. You do not want to be a pest or a pushy parent, and you certainly do not want to take over for your child because your child needs to learn how to do things for him- or herself. But you do want to make sure that the teachers understand your child's needs and are trying to address these issues.

Give your child a chance to settle in. After a few weeks, talk to him to see how he thinks things are going. Is he comfortable asking questions in class? Does he feel as if he understands the material? Can he find people to help him if he needs it? If your child is beginning to struggle, now is the time to address the issue, not months down the road when he or she is hopelessly behind and becoming more and more frustrated.

Schedule a conference with your child's teacher (and be sure to attend every regularly scheduled conference, even if you feel there are no pressing issues at the moment). Staying involved with and on top of your child's learning can make the classroom experience better.

Your job is to act as a translator for your child. He may not be able to express his concerns, so it is up to you to figure out what he needs. The teacher can help you with this. If something is not working, the two of you can work together to come up with a plan to enhance your child's comprehension. Sometimes, you will have to come up with more than one plan until you find something that works the best. Do not give up. Keep trying.

It may not be easy, but eventually, you may find something that seems to work well for your child. And years from now, your early work will all be worth it, for you will have a child who graduates from school confident about his abilities and whose self-esteem is high.

Chapter 16
Gifted Children

What do you do if your child shows exceptional ability in a certain area—whether academic, artistic, linguistic, or athletic? What if you feel that his or her needs will be better addressed in a private school where there will be more individual attention, more flexibility in teaching, more challenges, or a more nurturing environment?

You might want to begin by looking for specific schools that enroll students like your child. There are sports academies, schools for academically gifted students, music schools, drama schools, arts schools, and language schools. But, even if you live in an urban area, you may find that these schools are far away. You will have to consider whether or not you want your child to board (if that is a possibility) or whether you would prefer to find another alternative closer to home.

Many private schools look for children who are exceptional in certain areas. These are the types of students they most want to enroll. So if you do enroll your child in such a school, you will know that he or she will be taught to accept others, including their strengths and weaknesses, and you will know that others will value your child for his or her strengths and weaknesses. She probably won't be the only child with a high IQ who likes to study or the only musically gifted child or the only exceptional athlete. Private schools look for diversity and talent.

If your child is academically gifted, say reading at age four, possessing the vocabulary of a child many years older, solving difficult math problems or puzzles, and so on, you may want to find a school that is capable of challenging your student. Even if there are no schools specifically aimed at academically gifted children, you may find that a local private school is equipped to fulfill your child's needs. Especially if you live in a college town, you might find that many of the students at the local private school(s) are children of professors with degrees from Harvard and other top institutions. Your child might be surrounded by other children who are also academically gifted and by teachers who know how to nurture and challenge such students. It may not be necessary to find a school specifically aimed at gifted children.

If your child is gifted, you will likely want to find a school that has a small student-teacher ratio, so the teacher can spend time individually with your student and prepare appropriate lessons. The teacher should also be easily available to answer questions.

Many private schools know students have different learning styles, and they try to address these needs. They try to make students aware of how they learn, so the students can learn to make the most of their time. If students are exceptionally advanced, they may point them to an online course, which the teacher will, of course, help the student with. Even though the student is advanced, he or she may still have questions about the material and may need instruction from a teacher.

Many private schools have independent studies, where students can pursue a topic in detail that interests them. Some even have year-long projects, where students choose a topic, research it, narrow the focus, write a long report, and then prepare a thirty-minute presentation on what they have learned. A drama teacher may help the student prepare and practice the oral presentation.

Some schools have a gifted and talented coordinator, who focuses exclusively on the needs of these students. Talk to this person. Find out what they can provide for your child. Discuss your child's unique needs and learning styles. If there is not a gifted and talented coordinator, then talk to the head of the school. He or she should be able to discuss with you techniques they use to meet the needs of gifted students.

School Provisions
That Help Gifted Students

Here are some school provisions that can often help gifted students. Find out which of these the school has practiced in the past, how they worked, and whether or not they would consider using them in the future.

- **ability grouping,** where advanced students are grouped together and progress more rapidly than other groups. Research suggests that this can be particularly effective for gifted students.
- **acceleration/flexible progression.** Acceleration occurs when a student is more advanced in an area than his peers, and teachers tailor materials to the student or put the student in a more advanced class. Flexible progression allows students to work at their own level rather than at the level of others in their grade.
- **curriculum compacting,** where students cover, say, a year's worth of math in several months. Teachers first test to find out what students already know, and then they don't waste time reteaching this material. The technique generates time for extension activities, independent projects, and mentoring.
- **curriculum differentiation,** promotes a similar curriculum for all students, but varies task complexity, pacing, and avenues to learning based on student needs and abilities.
- **independent learning,** where students choose projects to extend the curriculum (either independently or in small groups).
- **mentoring,** where a student is paired with an older student or adult. Mentors act as advisers, consultants, and role models.

- **vertical unitized timetabling,** vertical grouping is when students of different ages work together based on their interests, learning speed, learning style, and so on. Unitized timetabling involves splitting the normal curriculum into smaller units that can be taken separately. Students can also combine units to join two or more curriculum areas together (to create a class, say, on the mathematics of music).

Curriculum Differentiation

For gifted students, curriculum differentiation means that teachers

- remove already mastered material from the curriculum
- add new content or product expectations to existing curriculum
- provide enrichment activities
- provide course work for able students at an earlier age than usual
- write new units or courses that meet the needs of gifted students.

Topics to Discuss

You may also want to discuss some or all of the following with the head of the school:

- the school's guidelines for acceleration
- teacher training regarding gifted and talented youngsters
- whether parent/teacher interviews are frequent
- how children are put into classrooms (by ability, by the best mix of learning styles, by finding a good mix of outgoing and inner-directed students, by a mix of energy levels, alphabetically, and so on)

- how they treat children who get distracted in noisy environments or large groups
- how they treat children who are very social when they need to work independently
- whether the school has a hands-on learning style or a lecture format
- what after-school activities the school has to support your child's interests

After you have discussed these issues and visited the school, you should have a sense of whether or not the school will work for you and your child. If you have concerns about the school, be sure to talk to someone about them now. Do not wait until your child is enrolled and then hope to change the direction of the school. This is usually not something that one person can accomplish.

Some schools do have a board of parents who are very active in deciding the direction of the school. Other schools have boards that do not have much power. If you are interested in influencing the direction of the school, you should find out how much clout the board has and how difficult it is to become a member of the board. And remember, if you do become a member of the board, you should expect to work hard. Becoming a board member is a position that is usually quite time consuming. If you do not have the time to devote, you should probably not consider becoming a board member.

Chapter 17
Boarding School? You've Got to Be Kidding!

Boarding schools are usually high schools, but sometimes they enroll middle school students. These schools are private college preparatory schools where students live on campus. At some schools, students go home on weekends; at others, most students stay seven days per week.

Why Are Boarding Schools Attractive?

The teachers and staff at boarding schools work hard to make sure the atmosphere is fun, safe, and academically challenging. Boarding schools are known for their academics. Students who attend boarding schools do more homework than other students. They also participate in sports more hours per week, watch less television, and play fewer video games. Boarding school students are well prepared for college because not only do they have the academic skills to succeed, but they also know how to schedule their time and provide for their own needs. Students at boarding schools learn personal responsibility, how to manage their time, leadership skills, moral values, and independence.

Because students and faculty live together twenty-four hours per day, teachers and staffers are able to squeeze teachable moments out of activities all day long—in the classroom, the eating hall, the dormitory, or the playing fields.

In addition, families who feel that their local high schools are unsafe, too large, unfriendly, anonymous, or unengaging may be interested in boarding schools. Parents sometimes feel that public schools force students to grow up too fast but that boarding schools do not have this pressure. At boarding schools, students have time to develop their academic, artistic, athletic, and social skills.

Types of Boarding Schools

There are several types of boarding schools. Your first step will be to decide which type of school is right for you.

Traditional Boarding School A traditional boarding school has all students living on campus all week long.

Boarding-Day School At this type of school, some students live in dormitories, while other students commute to school for the day and go home in the evening. If you are considering such a school, it is important to find out how many students will actually be around at night and on weekends. If most students do not stay, your student might be lonely if he stays.

Five-Day Boarding School At these schools, students can decide to go home on the weekends. It's important to find out how many students actually stay on campus over the weekend if your student plans to stay. Or if your student plans to commute home on the weekends, it is important to find out if he or she will be missing important opportunities.

Military School These schools often require uniforms and drill practices. They have a military structure, and some of the graduates go on to military colleges.

Junior Boarding School A junior boarding school accepts students who are in grades lower than high school. Most schools accept middle school students in grades six through eight, but some accept even younger students.

Preprofessional Arts School These schools specialize in training up-and-coming artists in musical, performing, or visual arts fields.

Religious School A religious school is affiliated with a specific religion, and religious education if often an important part of each school day.

What Next?

After you've decided on which type of boarding schools you would like to investigate further, what do you do? What if they are too far away to visit easily. Your best bet is to begin your research online. Try these web sites:

- http://www.schools.com
- http://www.nais.org

At these sites, you can search for schools by type, by region, by course offerings, and so on.

Next you will want to visit the web site of each school that you think has potential. You may also want to send off for a view book and information packet about the school. Using these resources, you may be able to answer these questions about each school:

- What is the school's philosophy?
- Where do the students come from? How many students are international students?
- What are the academics like?
- Is the environment nurturing? competitive? structured?
- Where is the school? How often will my student be able to come home?
- How large is the school?
- What extracurricular activities are available? Are they mandatory?
- Is the school equipped to teach students with learning difficulties or gifted students (or students with your child's unique needs)?

- What is the campus like on weekends?

After you have answered these and other questions you have, you may decide that you want to apply to one or more schools. Like applying to a day school, you will have to make a list of deadlines. In addition, you will need to make arrangements to travel to the school for visits and interviews. If the school is far away, this can present some difficulties, but it is best to visit the school at least once during the day and once on the weekend, so you can see how the school feels at these very different times.

If traveling is difficult, you can arrange for telephone interviews, but you should avoid this if at all possible. You will get a much better feel for the school if you visit, and the school will get a much better feel for your child. Visiting the school works to everyone's advantage.

When you visit the school, you will probably want to ask yourself the following questions:

- What are the dorms, campus, eating facilities, athletic fields, art rooms like?
- How happy do the students seem?
- Are people friendly and helpful to you?
- Are the students poised and helpful? rushed and stressed? happy and enthusiastic?
- Are the faculty and staff warm? helpful? approachable?
- What do students do in their spare time? Do they have spare time?
- How easy is it to stay in touch with family and friends back home? Are cell phones allowed? When? Are there opportunities to send email? When?
- Are there towns or restaurants nearby? Are students allowed to go into town or eat at off-campus restaurants?

- How safe is the surrounding community? Are students allowed to go places off campus alone?
- How much of the day is spend studying? How much pursuing athletics or special interests?
- Is there enough time to socialize? to complete homework? to talk to family and friends? to be alone?
- Do students get enough sleep?

The application process to a boarding school follows a schedule similar to the one for other types of private schools discussed in the previous chapters of this book. What makes the boarding school application process unique is that you are looking at schools that might be far away. Think carefully how being away from home will affect your child. Some students suffer from homesickness more than others. Most children get over their homesickness quickly, however, as they become familiar with new routines and make new friends and find adults to confide in. Most students come home from boarding school happy, mature, self-confident, and independent.

Chapter 18
Help! How Do I Pay for This?

There's no doubt about it, a private school education can be costly. But most people can and do find a way to pay for it. First of all, you should think about ways to tighten your belt. Do you really need to trade in your car, or can you continue driving it for a few more years? Do you really need to take that vacation to Hawaii? Maybe a camping vacation will be just as fun. Maybe staying in town for the summer and exploring museums, historical buildings, and local swimming holes will be pleasant and relaxing.

Second, think about ways to increase your income. Are you and your spouse both fully employed? Can you take on some additional work, freelance, or get a part-time job?

Third, look into financial aid options at the school to which you have applied. Most schools award need-based financial aid (and a few even offer merit-based financial aid). How large the financial aid offer is will vary—sometimes greatly—by school. Some schools have larger endowments and higher tuitions. These sources of funds help subsidize scholarships.

Qualifying for Financial Aid

To qualify for financial aid, you will have to fill out the Parents' Financial Statement (PFS) and mail it to the School and Student Service for Financial Aid (SSS) in Princeton, New Jersey. (A few schools do not use the PFS. If your school doesn't, find out what forms they use.) The PFS takes about eight hours to fill out, so plan accordingly. Don't expect to complete it the evening before it is due.

Some schools offer classes or information about filling out these forms. Take one of these classes, if available. The class will offer you insights on how aid is determined. (For example, you are not expected to apply money in a retirement account toward tuition, but a percentage of the monies in savings accounts or brokerage accounts is expected to be applied toward your child's tuition. It may be possible to move some money from a savings account into a retirement account to qualify for aid.)

If you own your own house and it has appreciated greatly in value since you bought it, it may be hard to qualify for aid. The appreciation in your home is considered an asset when calculating how much you can afford to pay. But it's not money most people can readily access unless they borrow against it. You may not want to put yourself this deeply in debt, especially if your child is only four years old and has fourteen years of private school ahead. If your child is entering high school, then a second mortgage may be a viable option, since these mortgages tend to have low rates.

In addition to funding from the school itself, other local sources may provide scholarship money. Begin by asking at your place of employment, your church, and local civic organizations. Your Chamber of Commerce or library might have information on local companies that provide scholarships to deserving students.

Most schools can put you in touch with companies that make tuition loans. These loans generally have low interest rates, and many loan companies will also provide financial aid counseling, so you will know what you are getting into before you sign on the dotted line.

Most schools also have tuition payment plans. Many of these plans allow you to spread the school's tuition payments out over twelve installments once a month. This is helpful if you cannot pay the tuition in one or two large installments. These plans usually charge a small fee to set up ($25 to $50), but can make payments more manageable. Many of these plans will set you up with an online account and let you make electronic payments from your bank account or credit card.

Sometimes it is easiest to use a credit card to pay a school's tuition, especially if your credit card company has some sort of a reward program, and you pay off the debt quickly. If you do not pay off the debt quickly, however, the reward will be more than offset by the interest you pay on the loan.

Financial Aid Resources

Some sources that can help you in your search or provide scholarships are listed below:

Independent School Alliance for Minority Affairs
1545 Wilshire Blvd, Suite 711
Los Angeles, CA 90017
213-484-2411

A Better Chance
88 Black Falcon Avenue, Suite 250
Boston, MA 02210-2414
617-421-0950
http://www.abetterchance.org
A Better Chance identifies highly motivated students of color who are at or above grade level and who demonstrate leadership potential. The organization refers these students to top private and public schools. The organization does not provide scholarships, but it does advocate for placement and financial aid.

School and Student Service for Financial Aid
609-406-5380
https://sss.ets.org

Assesses how much a family can afford to pay toward a private school tuition. Actual scholarship amounts are determined by individual schools.

The Children's Scholarship Fund (CSF)
http://www.scholarshipfund.org
The Children's Scholarship Fund provides partial tuition assistance for low-income families to send their children to private schools.

The Black Student Fund
3636 16th Street NW, 4th floor
Washington, D.C. 20010-1146
http://www.blackstudentfund.org
202-387-1414
Northern Virginia: 703-506-3552
email: mail@blackstudentfund.org
Provides financial assistance to Washington, D.C.-area African-American students in grades prekindergarten to twelve (70 percent of students are from one-parent families).

The Steppingstone Academy
155 Federal Street, Suite 800
Boston, MA 02110
617-423-6300
fax: 617-423-6303
email: info@sf.org

230 South Broad Street, Suite 1102
Philadelphia, PA 19102
215-599-0353
fax: 215-599-0357

http://www.tsf.org

With schools in Boston and Philadelphia, the Steppingstone Academy prepares motivated, urban students to get into and succeed at top independent schools and public exam schools. Students are accepted in fourth to seventh grades and attend new schools in sixth to ninth grade.

Glossary

boarding school a school where students do not return home daily. At some boarding schools, students return home on the weekends, but at others, students live on campus for the entire school year (except for school vacations).

boarding-day school a school at which some students live in dormitories, while other students commute to school for the day and go home in the evening.

charter school a school created by a legal charter and that is not usually controlled by the local school district. These are publicly funded schools that operate much like private schools.

coed school a school that admits both boys and girls, usually in equal numbers (as opposed to a boys' school or a girls' school, which enrolls students of only one gender).

day school a commuter school where students arrive in the morning for their classes and return home every evening (as opposed to a boarding school, where students spend both days and nights on campus).

five-day boarding school a boarding school at which students can decide to go home on the weekends.

independent school a school that is not affiliated with any religion or state agency, and, therefore, receives no money from taxes or a church. These schools are often some of the most academically challenging schools in the nation. They are usually governed by an independent board of trustees and make independent decisions about their mission, coursework, students, and faculty. Most belong to the National Association of Independent Schools (NAIS). These schools use tuition, gifts, and perhaps an endowment to pay operating expenses.

junior boarding school a boarding school that admits students beginning in middle school (and occasionally even younger).

military school a boarding school at which students receive some military training, may wear uniforms, where structure, discipline, physical fitness, military history, and strategy are emphasized. Sometimes graduates go on to military colleges.

Montessori school In 1896, Maria Montessori became the first female physician in Italy. Ten years later, she gave up her medical practice to work with young children. Her scientific observations led her to develop the Montessori method. Some features of a Montessori education include the following:

- Children normally stay in the same class for three years. Each child learns at her own pace.
- Hands-on learning is emphasized.
- Each manipulative has a step-by-step procedure for being used and focused toward a specific learning concept.
- Children learn everyday tasks such as pouring, sweeping, and tying.
- The curriculum emphasizes sight, sound, touch, taste, and smell.

parochial school a school that is managed and controlled by the Catholic Church, and that usually has nuns or priests among the teachers.

preprofessional arts school a school that specializes in training up-and-coming artists in musical, performing, or visual arts fields.

prep school a high school that is designed to prepare a student academically for college. Many prep schools are highly selective and accept only a small percentage of applicants. College preparatory schools often offer Advanced Placement courses, rigorous instruction, and small classes. Prep school graduates are often actively recruited by colleges because the colleges know these students will be well prepared for college academics.

private school a school that is independent of federal or state control. About 75 percent of private schools in the United States are run by churches or religious organizations. The other 25 percent have no religious affiliation, and often refer to themselves as independent schools.

religious school a school that offers a traditional academic program as well as daily or weekly courses in religion, requires regular church attendance during school hours, and emphasizes moral values. Some religious schools are controlled by a church and will have clergy among the teachers. Others are not church-controlled and have their own directors or trustees and few teachers who are clergy members.

semester school a boarding school that offers a specialized curriculum—such as language instruction in another country, oceanography, specialized science, sports instruction—for a semester only (usually to high school students).

trade school a private school at which students learn skills in a trade or vocation in which they intend to make a living as adults. Trade schools include beauticians' schools, automotive-repair schools, music schools, and performing arts schools.

Waldorf school Rudolf Steiner (1861 to 1925) created the method of instruction common to Waldorf schools. Some features of a Waldorf education include the following:

- There is no academic content in kindergarten, and minimal academics in first grade. Reading is not taught until second or third grade.
- From grades one to eight, students have one teacher who stays with the same class for the entire eight years.
- Art, music, gardening, and foreign languages (usually two in elementary grades) are central. All children learn to play the recorder and to knit.
- There are no textbooks in the first through fifth grades. Children have workbooks that they fill in during the year.
- Learning is noncompetitive. No grades are given in elementary school.
- The use of television and computers by young children are discouraged.
- The main subjects are taught for two to three hours per day for three to five weeks.

Resources

Independent Schools

**The National Association
of Independent Schools (NAIS)**
1620 L Street, NW
Washington, DC 20036-5605
202-973-9700
http://www.nais.org

Great Schools
965 Mission Street, Suite 500
San Francisco, CA 94103
415-977-0700
http://www.greatschools.net

Council for American Private Education
13017 Wisteria Drive, #457
Germantown, MD 20874
301-916-8460
http://www.capenet.org

**National Independent Private
School Association (NIPSA)**
10134 SW 78th Court
Miami, Florida 33156
305-630-2557
http://www.nipsa.org

The National Private Schools Association
3605 Sandy Plains Road, Suite 240-264

Marietta, GA 30066
800-840-0939, ext. 4
407-522-0214
fax: 407-298-3703
http://www.npsag.com

American Montessori Society
281 Park Avenue South, 6th floor
New York, NY 10010-6102
212-358-1256
http://www.amshq.org/schools.htm

Association of Waldorf Schools of North America
3911 Bannister Road
Fair Oaks, CA 95628
916-961-0927
fax: 916-961-0715
http://www.awsna.org
email: awsna@awsna.org

The National Coalition of Girls' Schools (NCGS)
228 Main Street
Concord, MA 01742
978-287-4485
http://www.ncgs.org

Association of Military Colleges and Schools of the United States
9429 Garden Court
Potomac, MD 20854-3964
301-765-0695
http://www.amcsus.org

The Association of Boarding Schools (TABS) Directory
4455 Connecticut Avenue, NW, Suite A200
Washington, DC 20008
202-966-8705
fax: 202-966-8708
http://www.schools.com

Peterson's Private Schools
http://www.petersons.com/pschools

U.S. Schools Online
http://privateschool.about.com/od/usschoolsonline

Religious Schools

Association of Christian Schools International
731 Chapel Hills Drive
Colorado Springs, CO 80920-1027
719-528-6906
http://www.acsi.org

Christian Schools International
3350 East Paris Avenue, SE
Grand Rapids, MI 49512-3054
616-957-1070
800-635-8288
fax: 616-957-5022
email: info@csionline.org
http://www.gospelcom.net/csi

National Catholic Educational Association
1077 30th Street, NW, Suite 100
Washington, DC 20007-3852
202-337-6232
http://www.ncea.org

Catholic Boarding Schools Association
5901 North 500 East
Rolling Prairie, IN 46371-0007
800-777-2697
http://www.cbsa.org

Network of Sacred Heart Schools
860 Beacon Street
Newton Centre, MA 02459
617-244-9260

http://www.sofie.org

Parochial School Directory
130 37th Street, NW
Auburn, WA 98001
253-735-2540
http://www.parochial.com

Catholic USA
http://www.catholicusa.com/
Includes a list of Catholic elementary schools, high school
schools, and colleges.

Catholic Online
http://www.catholic.org/clife/catholic_schools/

National Association of Episcopal Schools
815 Second Avenue, Suite 313
New York, NY 10017
800-334-7626
212-716-6134
fax: 212-286-9366
info@episcopalschools.org
http://www.naes.org

Southwestern Association of Episcopal Schools
1420 4th Avenue, Suite 29
Canyon, TX 79015-3751
806-255-2400
866-655-SAES (7237)
Fax: (806) 655-2426
http://www.swaes.org

The Council for Spiritual and Ethical Education
220 College Avenue, Suite 312
Athens, GA 30601
800-298-4599
fax: 678-623-5634
email: info@csee.org
http://www.csee.info

Resources by State

Alabama
Alabama Association of Independent Schools
106 Maple Street
Pisgah, AL 35765-6894
Phone: (256) 451-6019
Fax: (256) 451-6019

Southern Association of Independent Schools
1866 Southern Lane
Decatur, GA 30033-4033
Phone: (404) 633-2203
Fax: (404) 633-2433
http://www.sais.org

Alaska
Pacific Northwest Association of Independent Schools
5001 California Avenue, SW
Suite 112
Seattle, WA 98136
Phone: (206) 323-6137
Fax: (206) 324-4863
http://www.pnais.org

Arizona
Arizona Association of Independent Schools
c/o The Tesseract School
4800 East Doubletree Ranch Road
Paradise Valley, AZ 85253
Phone: (480) 991-1770
Fax: (480) 991-1954

Independent Schools Association of the Southwest
4700 Bryant Irvin Court, Suite 204
Fort Worth, TX 76107-7645
Phone: (817) 569-9200
Fax: (817) 569-9103
http://www.isasw.org

California
California Association of Independent Schools
1351 Third Street, Suite 303
Santa Monica, CA 90401
Phone: (310) 393-5161
Fax: (310) 394-6561
http://www.caisca.org

Western Association of Schools and Colleges (WASC)
533 Airport Blvd., Suite 200
Burlingame, CA 94010-2009
(650) 696-1060
http://www.acswasc.org

Colorado
Association of Colorado Independent Schools
714 Sugar Mill Avenue
Longmont, CO 80501-4013
Phone: (303) 702-0427
Fax: (303) 265-9776
http://www.acischools.com

Connecticut
Connecticut Association of Independent Schools
P.O. Box 159

12 Water Street
Mystic, CT 06355-0159
Phone: (860) 572-2950
Fax: (860) 572-2938

New England Association of Schools & Colleges: Commission on Independent Schools

209 Burlington Road
Bedford, MA 01730-1433
Phone: (781) 271-0022 x328
Fax: (781) 271-0950
http://www.neasc.org

Delaware
Association of Delaware Valley Independent Schools

701 West Montgomery Avenue
Bryn Mawr, PA 19010-3505
Phone: (610) 527-0130
Fax: (610) 527-4332
http://www.advis.org

Delaware Association of Independent Schools

P.O. Box 888
Hockessin, DE 19707
Phone: (302) 239-5263
Fax: (302) 239-5389

Florida
Florida Council of Independent Schools

1211 N. Westshore Boulevard, Suite 612
Tampa, FL 33607-4600
Phone: (813) 287-2820

Fax: (813) 286-3025
http://www.fcis.org

Southern Association of Independent Schools
1866 Southern Lane
Decatur, GA 30033-4033
Phone: (404) 633-2203
Fax: (404) 633-2433
http://www.sais.org

Georgia
Atlanta Area Association of Independent Schools
2647 Johnson Road, NE
Atlanta, GA 30345-1719
Phone: (404) 636-3023
Fax: (404) 633-8387
http://www.spx.org

Georgia Independent School Association
P.O. Box 1505
Griffin, GA 30224-0036
Phone: (770) 227-3456
Fax: (770) 412-0877
http://www.gisa-schools.org

Southern Association of Independent Schools
1866 Southern Lane
Decatur, GA 30033-4033
Phone: (404) 633-2203
Fax: (404) 633-2433
http://www.sais.org

Hawaii
Hawaii Association of Independent Schools
Ala Moana Pacific Center, Suite 1212
1585 Kapiolani Blvd.
Honolulu, HI 96814-4527
Phone: (808) 973-1540
Fax: (808) 973-1545
http://www.hais.org

Idaho
Pacific Northwest Association of Independent Schools
5001 California Avenue, SW, Suite 112
Seattle, WA 98136
Phone: (206) 323-6137
Fax: (206) 324-4863
http://www.pnais.org

Illinois
Independent Schools Association of the Central States
1550 North Dearborn Parkway
Chicago, IL 60610
Phone: (312) 255-1244
Fax: (312) 255-1278
http://www.isacs.org

Lake Michigan Association of Independent Schools
3760 N. Pine Grove
Chicago, IL 60613-4103
http://independentschools.net

Indiana
Independent Schools Association of the Central States
1550 North Dearborn Parkway
Chicago, IL 60610
Phone: (312) 255-1244
Fax: (312) 255-1278
http://www.isacs.org

Indiana Association of Independent Schools
Montessori Academy at Edison Lakes
530 E. Day Road
Mishawaka, IN 46545-3407
Phone: (574) 256-5313
fax: (574) 256-5493

Iowa
Independent Schools Association of the Central States
1550 North Dearborn Parkway
Chicago, IL 60610
Phone: (312) 255-1244
Fax: (312) 255-1278
http://www.isacs.org

Kansas
Independent Schools Association of the Southwest
4700 Bryant Irvin Court, Suite 204
Fort Worth, TX 76107-7645
Phone: (817) 569-9200
Fax: (817) 569-9103
http://www.isasw.org

Kentucky
Independent Schools Association of the Central States
1550 North Dearborn Parkway
Chicago, IL 60610
Phone: (312) 255-1244
Fax: (312) 255-1278
http://www.isacs.org

Kentucky Association of Independent Schools
c/o The Lexington School
1050 Lane Allen Rd
Lexington, KY 40504-2018
Phone: (502) 423-0440
Fax: (502) 423-0445

Southern Association of Independent Schools
1866 Southern Lane
Decatur, GA 30033-4033
Phone: (404) 633-2203
Fax: (404) 633-2433
http://www.sais.org

Louisiana
Independent Schools Association of the Southwest
4700 Bryant Irvin Court, Suite 204
Fort Worth, TX 76107-7645
Phone: (817) 569-9200
Fax: (817) 569-9103
http://www.isasw.org

Southern Association of Independent Schools
1866 Southern Lane
Decatur, GA 30033-4033
Phone: (404) 633-2203
Fax: (404) 633-2433
http://www.sais.org

Southwestern Association of Episcopal Schools
1420 4th Avenue, Suite 29
Canyon, TX 79015-3751
Phone: (806) 255-2400
Fax: (806) 655-2426
http://www.swaes.org

Maine
Association of Independent Schools
in New England
222 Forbes Road, Suite 106
Braintree, MA 02184
Phone: (781) 843-8440
Fax: (781) 843-3933
http://www.aisne.org

Independent Schools Association
of Northern New England
38 Clark Cove Road
Bowerbank, ME 04426-5308
Phone: (603) 775-7782
Fax: (603) 775-7792
http://www.isanne.org

Maine Association of Independent Schools
RR 1, Box 2600

Blue Hill, ME 04614
Phone: (207) 374-2808
Fax: (207) 374-2982

New England Association of Schools & Colleges: Commission on Independent Schools
209 Burlington Road
Bedford, MA 01730-1433
Phone: (781) 271-0022 x328
Fax: (781) 271-0950
http://www.neasc.org

Maryland
Association of Independent Maryland Schools
890 Airport Road, Suite I
Glen Burnie, MD 21061
Phone: (410) 761-3700
Fax: (410) 761-5771
http://www.aimsmd.org

Association of Independent Schools of Greater Washington
P.O. Box 9956
Washington, DC 20016-8956
Phone: (202) 625-9223
Fax: (202) 625-9225
http://www.aisgw.org

Massachusetts
Association of Independent Schools in New England
222 Forbes Road, Suite 106
Braintree, MA 02184

Phone: (781) 843-8440
Fax: (781) 843-3933
http://www.aisne.org

New England Association of Schools & Colleges: Commission on Independent Schools

209 Burlington Road
Bedford, MA 01730-1433
Phone: (781) 271-0022 x328
Fax: (781) 271-0950
http://www.neasc.org

Michigan
Association of Independent Michigan Schools

114477 Fredmar Road
Interlochen, MI 49643-0186
Phone: (231) 275-3506
Fax: (231) 275-3507
http://www.aims-mi.org

Independent Schools Association of the Central States

1550 North Dearborn Parkway
Chicago, IL 60610
Phone: (312) 255-1244
Fax: (312) 255-1278
http://www.isacs.org

Minnesota
Independent Schools Association of the Central States

1550 North Dearborn Parkway
Chicago, IL 60610

Phone: (312) 255-1244
Fax: (312) 255-1278
http://www.isacs.org

Mississippi
Southern Association of Independent Schools
1866 Southern Lane
Decatur, GA 30033-4033
Phone: (404) 633-2203
Fax: (404) 633-2433
http://www.sais.org

Missouri
Independent Schools Association
of the Central States
1550 North Dearborn Parkway
Chicago, IL 60610
Phone: (312) 255-1244
Fax: (312) 255-1278
http://www.isacs.org

Independent Schools of St. Louis
101 North Warson Road
Saint Louis, MO 63124-1326
Phone: (314) 567-9229
Fax: (314) 995-7451
http://www.independentschools.org

Missouri Independent School Association
Notre Dame de Sion
3823 Locust
Kansas City, MO 64109-2632
Phone: (816) 942-3282

Fax: (816) 942-4052
http://www.mocape.org/misa

**Missouri Council for American
Private Education (MO-CAPE)**
1911 Merlin Drive
Jefferson City, MO 65101
(573) 636-8659

Montana
**Pacific Northwest Association
of Independent Schools**
5001 California Avenue, SW, Suite 112
Seattle, WA 98136
Phone: (206) 323-6137
Fax: (206) 324-4863
http://www.pnais.org

Nebraska
**Independent Schools Association
of the Central States**
1550 North Dearborn Parkway
Chicago, IL 60610
Phone: (312) 255-1244
Fax: (312) 255-1278
http://www.isacs.org

Nevada
**Pacific Northwest Association
of Independent Schools**
5001 California Avenue, SW, Suite 112
Seattle, WA 98136

Phone: (206) 323-6137
Fax: (206) 324-4863
http://www.pnais.org

New Hampshire
**Independent Schools Association
of Northern New England**
38 Clark Cove Road
Bowerbank, ME 04426-5308
Phone: (603) 775-7782
Fax: (603) 775-7792
http://www.isanne.org

**New England Association of Schools & Colleges:
Commission on Independent Schools**
209 Burlington Road
Bedford, MA 01730-1433
Phone: (781) 271-0022 x328
Fax: (781) 271-0950
http://www.neasc.org

New Jersey
New Jersey Association of Independent Schools
629 Amboy Avenue
Edison, NJ 08837-3579
Phone: (732) 661-9000
Fax: (732) 661-9018
http://www.njais.org

New Mexico
**Independent Schools Association
of the Southwest**
4700 Bryant Irvin Court, Suite 204

Fort Worth, TX 76107-7645
Phone: (817) 569-9200
Fax: (817) 569-9103
http://www.isasw.org

New York
Association of Delaware Valley Independent Schools
701 West Montgomery Avenue
Bryn Mawr, PA 19010-3505
Phone: (610) 527-0130
Fax: (610) 527-4332
http://www.advis.org

New York State Association of Independent Schools
12 Jay Street
Schenectady, NY 12305-1987
Phone: (518) 346-5662
Fax: (518) 346-7390
http://www.nysais.org

North Carolina
North Carolina Association of Independent Schools
173 Tullyries Lane
Lewisville, NC 27023-9570
Phone: (336) 946-2819
Fax: (336) 945-0909
http://www.ncais.org

Southern Association of Independent Schools
1866 Southern Lane

Decatur, GA 30033-4033
Phone: (404) 633-2203
Fax: (404) 633-2433
http://www.sais.org

North Dakota
Independent Schools Association
of the Central States
1550 North Dearborn Parkway
Chicago, IL 60610
Phone: (312) 255-1244
Fax: (312) 255-1278
http://www.isacs.org

Ohio
Cleveland Council of Independent School
358 Applebrook Drive
Chagrin Falls, OH 44022-2687
Phone: (440) 893-9585
Fax: (216) 371-1501
http://www.ccis-ohio.org

Independent Schools Association
of the Central States
1550 North Dearborn Parkway
Chicago, IL 60610
Phone: (312) 255-1244
Fax: (312) 255-1278
http://www.isacs.org

Ohio Association of Independent Schools
P.O. Box 630
Sunbury, OH 43074-0630

Phone: (740) 965-2739
Fax: (740) 965-1373
http://www.oais.org

Oklahoma
Independent Schools Association of the Southwest
4700 Bryant Irvin Court, Suite 204
Fort Worth, TX 76107-7645
Phone: (817) 569-9200
Fax: (817) 569-9103
http://www.isasw.org

Oregon
Pacific Northwest Association
of Independent Schools
5001 California Avenue, SW, Suite 112
Seattle, WA 98136
Phone: (206) 323-6137
Fax: (206) 324-4863
http://www.pnais.org

Pennsylvania
Association of Delaware Valley
Independent Schools
701 West Montgomery Ave
Bryn Mawr, PA 19010-3505
Phone: (610) 527-0130
Fax: (610) 527-4332
http://www.advis.org

Pennsylvania Association of Independent Schools
37 E. Germantown Pike, Suite 302
Plymouth Meeting, PA 19462-1505

Phone: (610) 567-2960
Fax: (610) 567-2963
http://www.pais-papas.org

Rhode Island
Association of Independent Schools in New England
222 Forbes Road, Suite 106
Braintree, MA 02184
Phone: (781) 843-8440
Fax: (781) 843-3933
http://www.aisne.org

Independent Schools Association of Rhode Island
c/o Saint Michael's Country Day School
180 Rhode Island Avenue
Newport, RI 02840-3341
Phone: (401) 849-5970
Fax: (401) 849-7890

New England Association of Schools & Colleges: Commission on Independent Schools
209 Burlington Road
Bedford, MA 01730-1433
Phone: (781) 271-0022 x328
Fax: (781) 271-0950
http://www.neasc.org

South Carolina
Palmetto Association of Independent Schools
P.O. Box 4143
Greenville, SC 29608-4143
Phone: (864) 232-0003

Fax: (864) 232-0003
http://www.scpais.org

Southern Association of Independent Schools
1866 Southern Lane
Decatur, GA 30033-4033
Phone: (404) 633-2203 - Fax: (404) 633-2433
http://www.sais.org

South Dakota
Independent Schools Association
of the Central States
1550 North Dearborn Parkway
Chicago, IL 60610
Phone: (312) 255-1244
Fax: (312) 255-1278
http://www.isacs.org

Tennessee
Southern Association of Independent Schools
1866 Southern Lane
Decatur, GA 30033-4033
Phone: (404) 633-2203
Fax: (404) 633-2433
http://www.sais.org

Tennessee Association of Independent Schools
2014 Broadway, Suite 245
Nashville, TN 37203
Phone: (615) 321-2800
Fax: (615) 321-2827
http://www.taistn.org

Texas
Independent Schools Association of the Southwest
4700 Bryant Irvin Court, Suite 204
Fort Worth, TX 76107-7645
Phone: (817) 569-9200
Fax: (817) 569-9103
http://www.isasw.org

Southern Association of Independent Schools
1866 Southern Lane
Decatur, GA 30033-4033
Phone: (404) 633-2203
Fax: (404) 633-2433
http://www.sais.org

Utah
Pacific Northwest Association of Independent Schools
5001 California Avenue, SW, Suite 112
Seattle, WA 98136
Phone: (206) 323-6137
Fax: (206) 324-4863
http://www.pnais.org

Vermont
Independent Schools Association of Northern New England
38 Clark Cove Road
Bowerbank, ME 04426-5308
Phone: (603) 775-7782
Fax: (603) 775-7792
http://www.isanne.org

New England Association of Schools & Colleges: Commission on Independent Schools
209 Burlington Road
Bedford, MA 01730-1433
Phone: (781) 271-0022 x328
Fax: (781) 271-0950
http://www.neasc.org

Virginia
Association of Independent Schools of Greater Washington
P.O. Box 9956
Washington, DC 20016-8956
Phone: (202) 625-9223
Fax: (202) 625-9225
http://www.aisgw.org

Southern Association of Independent Schools
1866 Southern Lane
Decatur, GA 30033-4033
Phone: (404) 633-2203
Fax: (404) 633-2433
http://www.sais.org

Virginia Association of Independent Schools
6802 Paragon Place, Suite 525
Richmond, VA 23230-1644
Phone: (804) 282-3592
Fax: (804) 282-3596
http://www.vais.org

Washington State
Pacific Northwest Association
of Independent Schools
5001 California Avenue, SW, Suite 112
Seattle, WA 98136
Phone: (206) 323-6137
Fax: (206) 324-4863
http://www.pnais.org

Washington, D.C.
Association of Independent Maryland Schools
890 Airport Road, Suite I
Glen Burnie, MD 21061
Phone: (410) 761-3700
Fax: (410) 761-5771
http://www.aimsmd.org

Association of Independent Schools
of Greater Washington
P.O. Box 9956
Washington, DC 20016-8956
Phone: (202) 625-9223
Fax: (202) 625-9225
http://www.aisgw.org

West Virginia
Independent Schools Association
of the Central States
1550 North Dearborn Parkway
Chicago, IL 60610
Phone: (312) 255-1244
Fax: (312) 255-1278
http://www.isacs.org

Wisconsin
Independent Schools Association
of the Central States
1550 North Dearborn Parkway
Chicago, IL 60610
Phone: (312) 255-1244
Fax: (312) 255-1278
http://www.isacs.org

Wisconsin Association of Independent Schools
c/o Wayland Academy
101 North University Avenue
Beaver Dam, WI 53916-2253
Phone: (920) 885-3373 x240
Fax: (920) 887-3373
http://www.wayland.org

Wyoming
Pacific Northwest Association
of Independent Schools
5001 California Avenue, SW, Suite 112
Seattle, WA 98136
Phone: (206) 323-6137
Fax: (206) 324-4863
http://www.pnais.org

Financial Aid Sources

Independent School Alliance for Minority Affairs
1545 Wilshire Blvd, Suite 711
Los Angeles, CA 90017
213-484-2411

A Better Chance
88 Black Falcon Avenue, Suite 250
Boston, MA 02210-2414
617-421-0950
http://www.abetterchance.org
A Better Chance identifies highly motivated students of color
who are at or above grade level and who demonstrate
leadership potential. The organization then refers these
students to some of the nation's top private and public schools.
The organization does not provide scholarships, but it does
advocate for placement and financial aid.

School and Student Service for Financial Aid
P.O. Box 6662
Princeton, NJ 08541-6662
609-771-7770
https://sss.ets.org

The Children's Scholarship Fund (CSF)
8 West 38th Street, 9th floor
New York, NY 10018
212-515-7100
fax: 212-515-7111
email: info@scholarshipfund.org
http://www.scholarshipfund.org

The Children's Scholarship Fund provides tuition assistance to low-income families.

The Black Student Fund
3636 16th Street NW, 4th floor
Washington, D.C. 20010-1146
http://www.blackstudentfund.org
202-387-1414
Northern Virginia: 703-506-3552
email: mail@blackstudentfund.org
Provides financial assistance to Washington, D.C.-area African-American students in grades prekindergarten to twelve (70 percent of students are from one-parent families).

The Steppingstone Academy
155 Federal Street, Suite 800
Boston, MA 02110
617-423-6300
fax: 617-423-6303
email: info@sf.org

230 South Broad Street, Suite 1102
Philadelphia, PA 19102
215-599-0353
fax: 215-599-0357

http://www.tsf.org

With schools in Boston and Philadelphia, the Steppingstone Academy prepares motivated, urban students to get into and succeed at top independent schools and public exam schools. Students are accepted in fourth to seventh grades and attend new schools in sixth to ninth grade.

Children with Learning Difficulties

Schwab Learning
http://www.schwablearning.org
Among other things, this site lists schools by state. It also contains a host of other information that may be useful to a parent looking for a private school for their child with learning difficulties.

The Association of Boarding Schools (TABS)
4455 Connecticut Avenue, NW, Suite A200
Washington, DC 20008
202-966-8705
fax: 202-966-7808
http://www.schools.com
You can search the database for schools that work with students with ADD/ADHD, LD, or who need remedial instruction.

Peterson's Private Schools
http://www.petersons.com/pschools
The database of private secondary schools is searchable by key word. It also contains information about secondary schools for students with special needs.

National Association of Private Schools for Exceptional Children (NAPSEC)
1522 K Street, Suite 1032
Washington, DC 20005
202-408-3338
fax: 202-408-3340
http://www.napsec.com
email: napsec@aol.com

Provide NAPSEC with your child's profile and needs, either by phone or email, and they will search their member schools to identify which ones may be the best match for your child. They can do this nationally or by state, and it's free.

Parents for Residential Reform (PFRR)
http://www.pfrr.org
email: pfrr@fcsn.org
Hot Line: 800-872-9992 x199 or 617-723-8455 x199
Parents for Residential Reform is a grassroots organization of parents who have children in residential schools. The laws regarding residential programs are complex, and PFRR can guide parents through the maze that often includes DSS, DMR, DMH, DPH and the DOE.

International Dyslexia Association
Chester Building, Suite 382
8600 LaSalle Road
Baltimore, MD 21286-2044
410-296-0232
fax: 410-321-5069
http://www.interdys.org

Learning Disabilities Association of America
4156 Library Road
Pittsburgh, PA 15234-1349
412-341-1515
fax: 412-344-0224
http://www.ldanatl.org

National Center for Learning Disabilities
381 Park Avenue South, Suite 1401
New York, NY 10016
212-545-7510

fax: 212-545-9665
http://www.ld.org

Children and Adults with Attention Deficit Disorder

8181 Professional Place, Suite 150
Landover, MD 20785
800-233-4050
301-306-7070
fax: 301-306-7090
http://www.chadd.com

Gifted Children

American Association for Gifted Children (AAGC)
Duke University
Box 90270
Durham, NC 27708-0270
919-783-6152
http://www.aagc.org/

Davidson Institute for Talent Development
9665 Gateway Drive, Suite B
Reno, NV 89521
775-852-3483
fax: 775-852-2184
http://www.ditd.org
info@ditd.org

Hollingworth Center for Highly Gifted Children
827 Center Avenue #282
Dover, NH 03820-2506
207-655-3767
508-597-0977
http://www.hollingworth.org
Information and a newsletter on highly gifted children.

National Association for Gifted Children (NAGC)
1707 L Street, NW, Suite 550
Washington, DC 20036
202-785-4268
fax: 202-785-4248
http://www.nagc.org/

email: nagc@nagc.org
Advocacy organization; offers a wide range of publications and services.

National Conference of Governors' Schools
http://www.ncogs.org
email: info@ncogs.org
Information about summer programs for gifted and talented high school students.

The National Research Center on the Gifted and Talented
The University of Connecticut
2131 Hillside Road, Unit 3007
Storrs, CT 06269-3007
860-486-4676
fax: 860-486-2900
http://www.gifted.uconn.edu/nrcgt.html

Checklists
and
Worksheets

Contact Information Worksheet

School Name:

Admissions contact:

Title:

Address:

Address:

Phone:

Fax:

Email:

Financial Aid contact:

Title:

Address:

Address:

Phone:

Fax:

Email:

School Checklist

Name of School:

Item	Date Due	Date Completed
☐ Parent visit, tour, interview		
☐ Application and fee		
☐ Financial statement		
☐ Child visit		
☐ ISEE or SSAT scores		
☐ Family history form		
☐ Personal reference 1		
☐ School report		
☐ Teacher recommendation 1		
☐ Teacher recommendation 2		
☐ Child's essay		
☐ W-2s and tax forms		
☐ Admission letters mailed		
☐ Parent reply date		

Interview Deadlines Worksheet

Interviews must be completed by the following dates.

	Latest Date	**Date Completed**
School 1:		
School 2:		
School 3:		
School 4:		
School 5:		
School 6:		

Parent Tour Worksheet

School:
Address:
Contact/Phone:

Grades served (K to 8, 9 to 12):

Total number of students:

Total students in grade you are applying for:

Grade foreign language instruction begins:

Other instruction:

Extracurricular activities:

Extended day/after-school program:

Sports/athletics:

Facilities:

Arts instruction:

Teachers seemed:

Students seemed:

School seemed:

How school is unique:

Best qualities of school:

Worst qualities of school:

Teacher Recommendations Worksheet

Math Teacher Name:

Recommendations Needed at   Date Due   Date Sent

School I:

School 2:

School 3:

School 4:

School 5:

School 6:

English/Language Arts Teacher Name:

Recommendations Needed at   Date Due   Date Sent

School I:

School 2:

School 3:

School 4:

School 5:

School 6:

Personal References Worksheet

School 1   **Date Due**   **Date Completed**

Contact:
Phone Number:
Title:
School:
Address:
Address:
Notes:

School 2   **Date Due**   **Date Completed**

Contact:
Phone Number:
Title:
School:
Address:
Address:
Notes:

Letters of recommendation NOT needed for the following schools:

Student Visit Worksheet

School	Date	Time
School 1:		
School 2:		
School 3:		
School 4:		
School 5:		
School 6:		

No visit required at

Financial Aid Checklist

Name of School:
Phone Number/Contact Name:

Form	Date Due	Date Completed
❑ Parents' Financial Statement (PFS) to SSS in New Jersey		
❑ Copy of PFS to school		
❑ Preliminary financial aid application		
❑ Signed copy of IRS form 4506		
❑ Business/Farm Statement		
❑ Previous year's federal tax return and schedules and forms		
❑ Current federal tax return		
❑ W-2s and 1099s		
❑ School Scholarship form		
❑ After-school worksheet		
❑ Additional information		

Index

ABILITY GROUPING, 96

ACCELERATION/FLEXIBLE
PROGRESSION, 96

ACCEPTANCE LETTERS, 72
EARLY ACCEPTANCE
LETTERS, 68

ADMISSIONS TESTS, 53

ADVANTAGES OF PRIVATE
SCHOOLS, 2

APPLICATION, 39
BIOGRAPHICAL
INFORMATION, 40
HOW TO FILL OUT, 40
PHOTOGRAPH, 47

BOARDING SCHOOLS, 99
TYPES OF, 100

BUSINESS/FARM STATEMENT,
62

CHARTER SCHOOL, 109

CHECKLISTS, 149

CHILD VISIT, 56

CHILDREN WITH LEARNING
DIFFICULTIES, 143

COED SCHOOL, 109

CONTACT INFORMATION
WORKSHEET, IX, 15, 151

CURRICULUM COMPACTING, 96

CURRICULUM
DIFFERENTIATION, 96

DAY SCHOOL, 109

DECLINING OTHER OFFERS, 74

EDUCATIONAL TESTING
SERVICE (ETS)., 63

FINANCIAL AID, 56

APPLYING FOR, 61

COMPARING OFFERS, 72

QUALIFYING FOR, 104

RESOURCES, 106

SOURCES OF, 141

FINANCIAL AID CHECKLIST, 66,
158

GIFTED CHILDREN, 94
PROVISIONS THAT HELP, 96

HEALTH FORMS, 76

INDEPENDENT LEARNING, 96

INDEPENDENT SCHOOL, 109

INTERVIEW
CHILD, 58

INTERVIEW
PARENT, 25

INTERVIEW DEADLINES
WORKSHEET, 32, 153

ISEE, 54

JUNIOR BOARDING SCHOOL,
100

MENTORING, 96

MILITARY SCHOOL, 100

MONTESSORI SCHOOL, 9, 110

OPEN HOUSES, 18

PARENT INTERVIEW, 25
HOW TO DRESS, 25
QUESTIONS TO ASK, 28

PARENT TOUR, 33

PARENT TOUR WORKSHEET, 37,
154

PARENTS' FINANCIAL
STATEMENT (PFS), 61

PAROCHIAL SCHOOL, 11, 110, 117
PERSONAL REFERENCES WORKSHEET, 52, 156
PHONE LOG, 14
PREP SCHOOL, 111
PREPROFESSIONAL ARTS SCHOOL, 110, 111
PRIVATE SCHOOL, 111, 113, 115, 143
RELIGIOUS SCHOOL, 35, 101, 111, 116
RESOURCES, 113
  BY STATE, 119
  CHILDREN WITH LEARNING DIFFICULTIES, 143
  FINANCIAL AID, 106
  GIFTED CHILDREN, 146
  INDEPENDENT SCHOOLS, 113
  RELIGIOUS SCHOOLS, 116
ROLLING ADMISSIONS, 77, 79
SCHOOL AND STUDENT SERVICE FOR FINANCIAL AID (SSS), 104
SCHOOL CHECKLIST, 17, 152
SCHOOL PROVISIONS THAT HELP GIFTED CHILDREN, 96
SCHOOLS
  BOARDING, 100, 109
  BOARDING-DAY SCHOOL, 109
  CHARTER, 109
  COED, 109
  DAY, 109
  FIVE-DAY BOARDING, 109
  INDEPENDENT, 109
  JUNIOR BOARDING, 110

  MILITARY, 110
  MONTESSORI, 110
  PAROCHIAL, 110
  PREP, 111
  PREPROFESSIONAL ARTS, 111
  PRIVATE, 111
  RELIGIOUS, 111
  SEMESTER, 111
  TRADE, 111
  WALDORF, 112
SEMESTER SCHOOL, 111
SSAT, 53
STUDENT QUESTIONNAIRES, 53
STUDENT VISIT, 56
STUDENT VISIT WORKSHEET, 60, 157
STUDENTS WITH SPECIAL NEEDS, 88
SUMMER CAMP, 74, 82
SUMMER READING LISTS, 79
TEACHER RECOMMENDATIONS WORKSHEET, 50, 155
TRADE SCHOOL, 111
VERTICAL UNITIZED TIMETABLING, 97
WAIT LISTING, 70
WALDORF SCHOOL, 10, 112, 114
WORKSHEETS, 149
  CONTACT INFORMATION, 151
  INTERVIEW DEADLINES, 153
  PARENT TOUR, 154
  PERSONAL REFERENCES, 156
  STUDENT VISIT, 157
  TEACHER RECOMMENDATIONS, 155

Printed in the United States
99496LV00004B/96/A